'There my friends

The Strict Baptist Ch...   ...d

Nort...

Tim Grass

Thornhill Media

2012

My tongue repeats her vows,
Peace to this sacred house!
For there my friends and kindred dwell;
And, since my glorious God
Makes thee his blest abode,
My soul shall ever love thee well.

From the hymn 'How pleased and blest was I', by Isaac Watts (1674–1748), based on Psalm 122

Copyright © 2012 Tim Grass

First published in 2012 by Thornhill Media, 1 Thornhill Close, Ramsey, Isle of Man, IM8 3LA; tgrass.work@gmail.com

All rights reserved. No part of this publication may be reproduced, stored in a retrieval system, or transmitted in any form or by any means, electronic, mechanical, photocopying, recording or otherwise, without prior written permission from the publisher or a licence permitting restricted copying.

British Library Cataloguing in Publication Data
A catalogue record for this book is available from the British Library

ISBN: 978-0-9573190-0-4

Printed in the Isle of Man by Mannin Media, Douglas, Isle of Man

Contents

Acknowledgements	iv
Abbreviations	iv
Strict Baptists in Suffolk and Norfolk: A Brief History	1
Maps	15
Norfolk Chapels	17
Suffolk Chapels	49
Appendix 1: Membership Statistics, Suffolk and Norfolk Association	140
Appendix 2: Strict Baptist Places of Worship in Norfolk and Suffolk	141
Bibliography	155

Acknowledgements

I would like to thank all those who have provided me with information, loaned, e-mailed or donated material, allowed me to visit chapels, and assisted in so many other ways. The book would have been much longer in the making, and much shorter in reality, without the constant assistance of David and Sarah Woodruff of the library of the Strict Baptist Historical Society. Record offices in Bury St Edmunds, Ipswich, Lowestoft and Norwich have also provided a great deal of help, and I am also indebted to the staff of the Gospel Standard Library, Hove, and Dr Williams's Library, London. Particular thanks are also due to David Piper, administrator of the Association of Grace Baptist Churches (East Anglia), for allowing me to consult material in the care of that body. If I have failed to make appropriate acknowledgement of material used, please contact me and I will rectify this.

I would never have thought of producing this book if it had not been for the positive nature of my own upbringing among the churches meeting in these buildings; so it is only right that I express appreciation of the host of people who were part of that. Some may remember me as an awkward child, even if (or perhaps because) I was a pastor's son; this book may serve as an acceptable, if belated, apology!

Ramsey, Isle of Man

October 2012

Abbreviations

AGBC(EA)	Association of Grace Baptist Churches (East Anglia); formerly the Suffolk and Norfolk Association of Strict Baptist Churches
EV	*Earthen Vessel*
fl.	known to be in existence / active
G	*Grace Magazine*
GH	*Gospel Herald*
NRO	Norfolk Record Office, Norwich
SBHS	Strict Baptist Historical Society library, Dunstable
SBU	Suffolk Baptist Union [now incorporated in the Eastern Baptist Association]
SRO	Suffolk Record Office: (B) Bury St Edmunds, (I) Ipswich, (L) Lowestoft
TNA	The National Archives, Kew (formerly known as the Public Record Office)

An asterisk (*) against the title indicates that the chapel is a Grade II listed building; for further information about why it was listed, see www.britishlistedbuildings.co.uk.

Strict Baptists in Suffolk and Norfolk: A Brief History

In 1900, the moderator of the Suffolk and Norfolk Association of Particular Baptist Churches (as it was then called) expressed the view that 'If ever the religious history of Suffolk should be written, a long chapter will have to be devoted to our Association.' It never has been, in spite of the significance of these churches in the county's Nonconformist history. So, as it forms part of my own history, I was motivated to explore it further with the aid of a camera and parents with long memories of Strict Baptist life in the region. Visiting them, my father would sometimes ask, 'Which chapel are we going to today?' This book represents the firstfruits of that research, and I hope that at some point it will be possible to write a fuller history of the Strict Baptists in Suffolk and Norfolk. Readers with local knowledge may find errors as it has been out of the question to work through all the extant sources; moreover, I am not an architectural historian. Sometimes, too, it has been a fine judgement as to whether or not a particular congregation qualified for the designation 'Strict Baptist'; one or two may have been unjustifiably omitted. I shall therefore welcome any corrections and clarifications.

Why are these churches of interest? There are several reasons. Firstly, local and family historians often struggle to understand what has differentiated Strict Baptists from other Baptists. For that reason I have tried to include below some very basic explanation of what Baptists are, and how they viewed their buildings; my apologies to those who know these things already! Secondly, the great majority of the Strict Baptists of Suffolk in particular have traditionally been marked by a rather different ethos from that of many churches of the same label elsewhere in England. They have had more in common with the older Particular Baptist churches, and in particular a tradition of vigorous and outward-looking church life. Thirdly, an earlier historian of the denomination, Ralph Chambers, claimed that this 'is the only part of the Country where the principles of association among the churches have been continuously and successfully applied'.[1] His claim may have been overstated, but it contains a measure of truth. Finally, Strict Baptist history in Norfolk and Suffolk has often marked by a fairly high degree of ability to adapt to a particular host culture and to conduct their church life in a manner which offers an expression of that rather than a negation of it. This is not altogether surprising, since it can be claimed that one wing of the Strict Baptists as a distinct denomination originated in Suffolk.

Before going any further, let me explain the structure and contents of the book. There is a page, or a double-page spread, for each church, in alphabetical order for Norfolk and then Suffolk. Brief details of some branch chapels are included under the parent cause. The pictures focus on the chapels, but the accompanying text also sketches the history of the churches which met in them. For some churches, much fuller information is provided than for others. Records have not always survived; some causes have attracted the attention of later writers whereas others equally deserving have not; my own research could have been prolonged almost indefinitely, but a halt had to be called somewhere! Details of further reading are also provided, along with information about records known to be held by public institutions (including references to be quoted when inquiring about the items). I have not included full details of transcriptions of monumental inscriptions, but these should be fairly straightforward to trace through internet searching. You will notice that most registers of

---

[1] Ralph F. Chambers, 'The Strict Baptist chapels of England, Volume –: The Chapels of East Anglia: Covering the Counties of Suffolk, Norfolk, and Cambridgeshire' (typescript, n.d.), 1.

births, marriages and deaths ended around 1837; parliamentary legislation passed that year established a system of state registration of these events, and shortly afterwards Nonconformist registers were required to be deposited with the authorities. Appendix 1 gives membership statistics for churches belonging to the Suffolk and Norfolk Association, providing some indication of how congregations grew or declined. Appendix 2 lists all locations where regular services or other outreach activities are known to have taken place after 1830. This is not a complete listing of all sites of Baptist activities in these counties, but it does show how, where and when the Strict Baptists were active in church-planting.

Most functioning churches retain their own records, or at least the current ones; they may sometimes allow inquirers to consult them, but such permission should always be taken as a privilege rather than a right, not least because church records often contain information of a confidential nature. More often they will consult records on an inquirer's behalf. Moreover, church secretaries are not professional genealogists. However, they will often be glad to help where they can, especially if inquirers make things easier by giving as much background information as possible.

Early Baptist Work

Baptist congregations emerged in England during the early seventeenth century. There were two main types, Particular and General. These designations point to the differing views of the work of Christ on the cross: Particular Baptists believe that his atonement is effective for the elect only, those chosen by God to receive salvation; this is part of a Calvinistic understanding of salvation, which stresses human inability to respond to God apart from the gift of his grace, and the sovereignty of God in saving sinners. General Baptists believe that the atonement is potentially effective for all. Both, it must be said, have usually engaged in vigorous evangelistic outreach. Converts have been baptized as believers (incidentally, it is better to speak of 'believer's baptism' than 'adult baptism'), on profession of repentance for sin and faith in Christ, and almost from the beginning the usual mode of baptism has been by immersion, hence the need in their chapels for something other than the traditional font.

The requirement of a personal profession of Christian faith has meant that Baptist churches have been composed of those who have made a conscious choice to 'opt in', and so there has been a correspondingly high expectation of members to live a consistent Christian life, attend worship regularly and contribute to the work and finances of the church. Both types of Baptist have practised a form of church government which places primary responsibility for this, and for the funding of church work, on the local congregation. Their congregational emphasis was shared by the denomination known as Independents or Congregationalists, and not infrequently the two collaborated in Suffolk to establish mission stations. There are certain differences which have been evident during the course of Baptist history, but these need not concern us here, apart from the fact that Particular Baptist churches not infrequently organized themselves in regional associations. These provided a platform for conferring about difficulties and challenges, as well as a means of planning and resourcing the planting of new congregations.

The term 'Strict', by the way, refers not to lifestyle, which was neither more nor less strict than that advocated in other Baptist circles, but to the practice of restricting participation in the communion service (often known as 'the Lord's Supper') to those baptized by immersion as believers (and often, during the nineteenth century, to members of churches sharing the same faith and church order).

These believers did not regard infant sprinkling as true Christian baptism, and they understood the New Testament as teaching that since baptism belonged to the beginnings of the Christian life, along with repentance for sin and faith in Christ as the only Saviour, it was a prerequisite to communion, participation in which was reserved for Christian believers.

Baptist preachers were active in Norfolk and Suffolk during the Civil War and Commonwealth periods. In Norfolk several enduring churches were established, including Ingham (1653), Norwich (1669) and Great Ellingham (1699). In Suffolk, two Baptist churches appear to have existed during the later seventeenth century, at Framlingham and Lavenham, both died out early in the eighteenth century. There was a church at Bildeston, founded in 1737, which admitted Independents as well as Baptists to membership. But the earliest definite Particular Baptist church in Suffolk appears to have been that at Woolverstone, which came into being in 1757 as a daughter congregation of the church at Colchester (now Eld Lane); this moved in 1775 to Stoke Green, Ipswich. An offshoot was the church at Wattisham, formed in 1763.

It was at Shelfanger in Norfolk that the first steps were taken to form a regional association of Particular Baptist churches, the Norfolk and Suffolk Association, in 1769. Founding members were Claxton, Shelfanger and Worstead in Norfolk, and Woolverstone and Wattisham in Suffolk. By 1790, the *Baptist Annual Register* recorded churches in Norfolk at Claxton, Dereham, Diss, Great Ellingham, Ingham, Kings Lynn, Norwich (two), Shelfanger, Worstead and Great Yarmouth, but in Suffolk only at Ipswich and Wattisham (Bildeston was not listed, probably because it did not require believer's baptism as a prerequisite to communion). The association struggled to survive, as churches often remained independent for reasons which could be financial or doctrinal. It was during the unsettled decade of the 1790s, when the nation went to war with France amid fears of a French-style revolution this side of the Channel, and Dissenters were often suspected as potential traitors to the national interest, that the remarkable growth of Baptists in Suffolk began.

A postcard of Garland St Chapel, Bury (1834), which replaced a chapel in Nether Baxter St. This was the principal scene for the ministry of Cornelius Elven (1797–1873), and the mother church of most of the Strict Baptist causes in West Suffolk; but it never became a Strict Baptist church. The same was true of parent churches at Diss, Ipswich (Stoke Green) and Walton, near Felixstowe.

The Emergence of the Strict Baptists as a Distinct Grouping

By the late 1820s it was felt by some that the original principles on which the Norfolk and Suffolk Association had been founded were no longer being adhered to. This was a time of flux in Baptist circles, and the Calvinistic understanding of salvation which had energized late eighteenth-century preachers was subject to modification in significant respects (and in opposite directions: some toned it down to allow more stress on human responsibility to believe the gospel, while others sharpened it up to emphasize divine sovereignty). The same phenomenon was occurring, at the same time, in Scottish Presbyterianism.

Eleven churches withdrew from the old association, all in Suffolk (Bardwell, Beccles, Grundisburgh, Hadleigh, Halesworth, Horham, Rattlesden, Little Stonham, Southwold, Walton and Wattisham), of which six formed the new at Grundisburgh on 22 September 1829, signing a circular letter: Beccles, Hadleigh, Halesworth, Little Stonham, Rattlesden and Wattisham. In the letter, they explained that their secession had been precipitated by the growth of ideas which they saw as incompatible with the old association's doctrinal basis. George Wright of Beccles, the leading figure on the Strict Baptist side, offered his interpretation of events in a circular letter to the new association the following year.

> Some of the associated ministers appeared to us to err in countenancing sentiments contrary to the principles upon which our union was professedly founded, and to the doctrines of sovereign and discriminating grace; sentiments false in theory and baneful in their tendency, and against which we feel ourselves bound most earnestly to protest; - and as we are sensible that we have no right to affect the control of any man's judgment, we proposed that the several churches should be requested to consider whether it would not be advisable to come to an amicable division of the Association. The motion being objected to, it was withdrawn, lest by urging it we should provoke an unavailing contention: and as co-operation for the most important objects could not be consistently continued without unity of judgment, no other course was open to us but that which we have taken.[2]

Wright alleged that the ordinances of baptism and the Lord's Supper had not been preserved in purity. Ministers had been called whose testimony to an experience of God's grace was dubious, as was their call to the ministry; deacons had been chosen for their wealth or respectability; and members admitted who could give no account of the Holy Spirit's work in their lives. Communion was being 'profanely administered to the unbaptized, upon a principle of mistaken candour'.[3] But the practice of restricting communion to those baptized as believers, whilst it became a key difference between the two associations, was at this point a subsidiary issue.

Christian grace was shown on both sides, but it was a difficult time. Daniel Wilson, the pastor at Tunstall, recorded in 1830 after a meeting of the old association: 'Our association is also gone by, but far from comfortable. We are divided into two, and cannot walk together any longer, because we are not agreed. They divided upon Fullerism, and I am uncomfortably situated, for my mind is with the new association, and I expect my church will continue with the old'.[4]

---

[2] *Circular Letter on Christian Unity, by the Suffolk and Norfolk New Association of Baptist Churches …* (Bungay, 1830), p.4.
[3] *Circular Letter 1830*, p.18.
[4] Daniel Wilson, *The Life of Daniel Wilson, late Pastor of the Baptist Church, Tunstall, Suffolk* (Woodbridge, 1847-8), p.108. Very briefly, Fullerism was the view that it was the duty of all who heard the gospel to repent and believe; it was named after the Baptist theologian Andrew Fuller (1754-1815). Strict Baptists rejected this on the ground that saving faith was not a legal duty but something which only God could give. Both sides in the controversy agreed that the gospel was to be preached to all, but Fuller asserted in addition that faith was the duty of all. In 1807 the old association had issued a 'Testimony' against such views (which I have not traced), hence Wright's conviction that it had shifted its ground.

For many years the circular letters of the new association included a paragraph inside the front cover asserting that it had been founded in 1829 in order to maintain the faith and practice of the old association formed in 1771. The Suffolk and Norfolk was, however, the first association to incorporate the new and arguably higher form of Calvinistic theology alongside the practice of strict communion (by now being more widely questioned among Particular Baptists). Several others would appear in various parts of England, but they never quite matched its success. This was due in measure to the quality of its early leadership: George Wright, John Cooper and Samuel Collins, the triumvirate who led it for about half a century, were men who combined theological depth with a vigorous evangelistic outlook. Moreover, the churches felt a strong degree of responsibility for one another. Article 7 of the new association urged them to seek each other's prosperity and laid down that it would, when required, offer advice and do what it could to promote unity within a church (an indication, perhaps, of the frequency of disunity), subject to the independence of each local church. When a church lost its pastor, article 8 stipulated that it should 'be supplied once a month by the ministers of the associated churches, if required to do so; the church needing such assistance, shall first apply to the church which is nearest to it, and so proceed to others; and pay the travelling expenses of the several ministers supplying them'. A third factor giving coherence to the new grouping was a monthly magazine, the *Gospel Herald*, which first appeared in 1831. In time it was taken over by the Metropolitan Association of Strict Baptist Churches (formed in 1861), and it continued to appear until 1970, when it was incorporated into a new monthly, *Grace Magazine*.

This book limits its focus to the churches designated 'Strict Baptist' after 1830, and does not attempt to cover the Particular Baptist churches which did not form part of that community at any point. Had those been included, there would have been too many to look at; but more importantly the Strict Baptist churches, whilst conscious of their roots in the older Particular Baptist tradition, developed fairly distinct identities of their own over time, as well as the usual institutional networks created to give expression to it.

I use the plural 'identities' because there were a number of other Strict Baptist churches, mostly in Norfolk but a few in Suffolk, which did not form part of the new association, nor did they share its approach to evangelism and church planting. Many of these were associated with the *Gospel Standard* magazine, and these arguably constitute a separate denomination. Their origins were usually independent of the others, too; several appear to have arisen from the activity of William Huntington and his followers in and around the Fens (see Lakenheath). They were distinguished from other Strict Baptist churches by rejection of the idea that the moral law, as expressed above all in the Ten Commandments, formed the believer's rule of life (this emphatically did not mean that they condoned moral laxity or rejected the authority of Scripture and its moral teaching, simply that they regarded the believer as one who was saved through grace rather than law-keeping); by the denial that the all without distinction were to be exhorted to repent and believe; and in time also by insistence upon the doctrine that Christ was not only eternally divine, but eternally the Son of God. Their two main leaders nationally were the ex-agricultural labourer William Gadsby (1773–1844) and the former Anglican clergyman J.C. Philpot (1802–69). Gadsby preached at least once in Norwich, but neither is known to have preached elsewhere in Suffolk or Norfolk. Several Gospel Standard churches were formed, at Lakenheath, West Row, Downham Market, Southery, Kings Lynn, Norwich (Jireh and Zoar), Bungay and Lowestoft; the churches at Brooke and Fressingfield also aligned themselves with these churches for a period from the 1920s. But the ground in Suffolk was already thickly covered for the most part and the Particular Baptist churches found themselves out of sympathy with the more inward-looking spirituality of their Gospel Standard brethren and their rejection of the moral law. Moreover, unlike the churches founded by these two men, they were mostly very association-minded.

Outreach and Expansion

The historian of Suffolk Baptists, A.J. Klaiber, has asserted that the division in 1829 was a cause of decline in the Baptist evangelism, but the evidence appears to contradict this. The new association began in division, but, like the contention between Paul and Barnabas in Acts 15, it was a division which resulted in increased evangelistic activity. Strict Baptists shared to the full in the Particular Baptist vision to plant new congregations, and the methods adopted were similar. Many causes began as outreach from a mother church. By 1837, Baptists of all types in Suffolk had services in about 140 villages where they had no meeting house. Cornelius Elven, pastor of the church at Bury St Edmunds, was maintaining twenty himself in 1835, and although he did not become a Strict Baptist, a number of the churches which he founded did so. Looking back on the new association's first half-century, S.K. Bland asserted that 'the evidence of figures showed that those Churches generally maintaining the largest number of outlying preaching Stations had been favoured with the greatest increase'.[5] Cottages were licensed for worship, open air meetings were held, and before most churches installed baptisteries in their chapels, baptizing services provided perhaps the highest-profile evangelistic opportunity. These often drew crowds of over a thousand, although the presence of unsympathetic or drunk onlookers could create challenges for maintaining order.

Several agencies assisted Strict Baptist churches in outreach. There was the Suffolk and Norfolk Baptist Home Missionary Society, which began with a proposal from Samuel Collins at the annual meetings in 1831. By 1847 it was active in Suffolk, Norfolk, Cambridgeshire and Huntingdonshire. In 1871, men connected with it were preaching in a hundred villages. As late as 1931 it was supplying 42 stations, by then divided into 12 districts.

By 1862 the new association could report 103 village stations maintained by member churches, and a combined membership of over 3,000. Baptisms had peaked sharply at 218 in 1861, implying that the churches may have been more influenced by the religious revival affecting much of Britain from 1858 than might be thought from the printed evidence. The churches seemed in good health; but the area was to be affected by agricultural depression and the migration of many to larger centres of population, and the churches also by the growing availability of alternative forms of leisure activity and the impact of wider currents of thought which were inimical to traditional Christian beliefs.

Relations with the rest of the regional Particular Baptist community fluctuated. When the Suffolk Baptist Union was formed in 1846 (the old association was wound up in 1849), the Strict Baptist church at Stowmarket refused to lend their chapel for its inaugural meetings in 1848. However, things soon improved, and relations between the Suffolk and Norfolk Association and the Suffolk Baptist Union remained warm for much of the nineteenth century and beyond (there were few if any links with the Norfolk Baptist associations). Preachers moved between the two, as did churches, and it was not unknown for churches to support both foreign missionary societies (the Baptist Missionary Society and the Strict Baptist Mission), as indeed did the new association itself. Annual contributions were sent to the Baptist Union of England and Wales until at least 1880.

---

[5] *Circular Letter on 'Life in Christ:' by the Suffolk and Norfolk Association of Particular Baptist Churches ...* (Eye, 1879), p.23.

Such interchange gradually lessened from the 1860s onwards, a casualty of strained relationships following outspoken opposition by some to things held dear by Strict Baptists, in particular the practice of strict communion. A celebrated case in 1860 (involving St Mary's Baptist Church, Norwich) resulted in the legal judgment that this was not a fundamental part of Particular Baptist polity, thus accelerating the trend towards open communion in many churches with a Particular Baptist trust deed. Several Strict Baptist causes were formed around this time (Norwich, Gildencroft; Lowestoft, Tonning St; and Sudbury), as churches divided over the communion issue. Nevertheless, in Suffolk at least the two constituencies continued to interact, with each association sending messengers to bring greetings at the annual gathering of the other by 1900, a practice which continued until the 1980s.

In 1849 there were the following associations of Baptist churches in the two counties:

- East Norfolk and Norwich (14 churches, founded 1828, from 1834 known as the Norfolk & Norwich Association)
- West Norfolk (12, split 1847 from Norfolk & Norwich, reunited 1862)
- Friendly Union (an informal network, active by 1837, comprising Attleborough, Carleton Rode, Shelfanger and Kenninghall; by 1851 Diss and Great Ellingham had been added)
- Suffolk and Norfolk (30, founded 1829)[6]
- Suffolk Baptist Union (18, founded 1846; known 1849-1903 as the Suffolk & Norfolk Home Missionary Union)

There were also 35 churches unaffiliated with any association (in outlook these often corresponded to those in the Suffolk and Norfolk Association, and indeed a number later joined it), and 5 belonging to the New Connexion of General Baptists, which were not part of the Particular Baptist tradition. Among those which were unaffiliated, 'Gospel Standard' churches were also appearing.

The Annual Meetings

From the beginning, the new association held annual meetings at which sermons were preached and association business transacted; this was established practice among Baptists and Independents, and the two days of meetings were eagerly anticipated by many. They provided a feast of good things in terms of preaching, and a rare opportunity for like-minded believers from different churches to converse. Churches would take it in turn to host the meetings, which involved putting up large numbers of visitors, as well as catering for them between the services (extending sometimes to the provision of a tent for smoking!). Initially these meetings took place in the chapels, but as early as 1835 so many turned up that at least one service was held outdoors, a number of wagons being drawn up in a semi-circle in a meadow next to the chapel at Stonham, that year's host church. In 1846, therefore, it was resolved to purchase a tent in order to avoid the necessity of erecting expensive temporary booths to accommodate the congregation (as had first been done in 1819 at the old association's annual meeting at Shelfanger); first used in 1847, it could accommodate 2,000 standing worshippers. Gathering in a tent became a part of the mystique of these meetings.

---

[6] At several points the new association's name was altered. It was the Suffolk and Norfolk New Association of Baptist Churches until 1848, when the word 'New' was dropped. In 1854 it became an association of 'Particular Baptist Churches' and remained so until 1929, but in 1930 this was altered to 'Strict Baptist'.

By 1870, it was reported that as many as 3,500 were present. The meetings attracted large crowds until recent decades, and are again beginning to increase after some years of decline. They provided a feast of preaching, but for many 'the Association' was also a highlight of the annual social calendar.

Until World War II, the association's annual business meeting also took place during the meetings; now it is held some weeks before. This was where churches were admitted or their withdrawal formalized; where structures were set up to resource congregations in such matters as funds and outreach; and where resolutions were passed which dealt with matters of moment, denominationally or nationally. Thus a resolution was passed in 1871 calling for – and confidently anticipating – the disestablishment of the Church of England. Constant vigilance was exercised against perceived Anglican attempts to control the educational system and thus disseminate doctrinal error. In 1896 and 1902, resolutions expressed disapproval of education legislation then before Parliament, the concern being that children would be indoctrinated with high-church Anglican ideas as a result. Nonconformists of all shades were united in opposing this, partly because of their conviction that the message of salvation by faith in Christ was imperilled by Anglican emphasis on the sacraments. Rather than such sectarian teaching, they called for non-denominational and factually orientated Scripture instruction. (On the other hand, from the 1880s onwards thanks were being expressed to local Anglicans for providing hospitality for attenders at the tent meetings.) Other issues considered were usually matters of personal morality. In 1886 petitions were being sent to Parliament regarding the closure of public houses and places of amusement on the Lord's day.

It is difficult to over-estimate the role played by the tent meetings in fostering a sense of cohesion among the churches. By moving round the churches, especially those in out-of-the-way locations, they gave them all a sense of being part of something larger and dynamic.

Tea-tables at the 1914 Association (courtesy of AGBC(EA)

Church Life

A strong sense of cohesion was also evident within congregations, especially in rural areas. Between Sunday services, folk would eat lunch together. 'The practice of taking dinners to Chapel on Sundays has been one of the strongest factors in keeping rural congregations together in Suffolk.'[7]

---

[7] G.T. Botwright, *Those Hundred and Fifty Years: A Ter-Jubilee History of the Strict Baptist Church at Aldringham, Suffolk* (n.pl., 1962), p.9.

Intermarriage within the congregation was common, and marriage to those outside the faith a matter for discipline, during the nineteenth century at least. Close attention was paid by most churches to keeping the membership roll up to date: those ceasing to attend would have their membership withdrawn, as would any who fell into doctrinal error, ungodly ways or conduct which imperilled the church's peace and unity. Members were to lead lives which stood out from the world.

Most churches introduced Sunday Schools, which often catered for adults as well, teaching them to read. That such instruction was needed is evident from the church at Kenninghall: over half the members received during its first two decades could not write their own names. Concern for their children, whom members did not wish to be indoctrinated with Anglican teaching, meant that several churches also maintained day schools from the mid 1840s onwards.

By the 1860s concern was being expressed about the drift of population to the towns. In 1894 the Rishangles church reported that the population of their village had halved over fifty years; coupled with growing indifference to religious observance, the result was a serious decline in attendance. This would have been replicated elsewhere, although as yet membership figures did not show the same degree of decline: it was the 'hearers', those who attended worship but made no profession of personal faith, who were falling off.

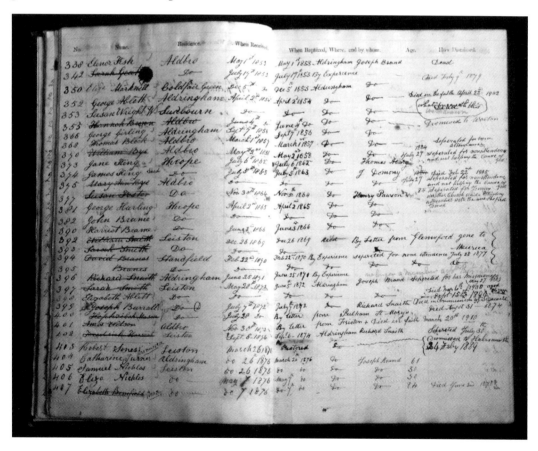

This book, from Aldringham, records the members received and what happened to them

The Buildings

First of all, let me distinguish the terms 'church' and 'chapel'. Until recent decades, the Christians described in this book have used the term 'church' to refer to the body of believers in Christ, whether a local congregation or the universal aggregate of all such believers at all times and in all places. Eighteenth-century Baptists spoke of their buildings as 'meeting houses', a designation still preserved in the road name 'Meeting Lane', found at Grundisburgh and elsewhere. Attending worship would often be described as 'going to meeting'. By the period covered here, the building in which the church met was referred to as the 'chapel' (often – but confusingly – contrasted with 'church', i.e. the Church of England, when describing a person's religious allegiance). Whilst it was treated as special because of its associations with the worship of God, it was not regarded as holy in itself; Baptists have no concept of 'consecrated buildings', which may help us to understand why many of the buildings featured here do not manifest specifically 'religious' architectural forms but share much in common with secular buildings of the same period and locality. All the same, it was felt necessary in 1913 to warn against the use of chapels for amusement, political meetings and other secular purposes, and 'also against the habit occasionally observable of allowing children to use the place of public worship as a kind of Sunday playground'![8]

Congregations almost always began by meeting in private homes or barns, certified for use for the purposes of public worship; to meet without such certification exposed participants to legal action by unsympathetic clergy or landowners. If work did not prosper, then such use might cease within a few months or years, although a repeat effort might be made. Sometimes work was undertaken to convert them for their new use. None now survive as places of worship.

The next step, once a stable congregation had been established and finances permitted, was to build a chapel. In a sense, the pictures can speak for themselves. But it is worth highlighting some common features. It should also be stressed that much about these chapels was shared by contemporary buildings of the Congregationalists and to some extent also the Methodists. Until the later nineteenth century, it is rare for us to know who designed a particular building. Indeed, even the term 'design' is perhaps an overstatement; these were functional edifices, put up by men who would have been familiar with what was needed to build a barn or a cottage. Yet they have their own beauty: their style blends with so much of the rest of the built landscape of rural Suffolk, and they are often accompanied by attractive and peaceful burial grounds. The poverty of many members, especially in rural congregations, hindered them in supporting pastors and upgrading premises. Ironically, this may have contributed to the survival of a number of earlier buildings in 'vernacular' styles whose value can now be recognized from an architectural viewpoint. This vernacular feel, along with the retention rather than replacement of many early buildings, makes them of interest.

Most are fairly prominent; few of these churches were in existence during that part of the eighteenth century when it was wise for Dissenters to keep a low profile. Some are situated outside the villages they served; that could have been because they were built near a road junction, because the land was cheap, or because a sympathetic landowner made a plot available. When a chapel was replaced by a larger one, it was often on the same site.

---

[8] *Circular Letter on 'Divine Worship,' its Essentials and its Need of Reverence, by the Suffolk and Norfolk Association of Particular Baptist Churches, 83rd Annual Meetings at Bradfield St. George, on May 28th and 29th, 1913* (Leiston, 1913), p.14.

Often the buildings have a hipped roof rather than gable end walls; the roof may be of red or black pantiles, like many local cottages, although slate was frequently used; none survive with thatched roofs. Brick was the most common building material, easily available locally, but in on the edge of the Fens there are several flint-faced chapels, and a few were built of clay lump. Some were able to afford an imposing gault brick frontage, perhaps with inset window bays and porches for the entrance doors. There is a marked lack of Gothic detailing, such as pinnacles or pointed arches to windows and doors, and you will look in vain for a tower or spire! Few Strict Baptist chapels aspired to ape Anglican churches, which is not surprising given their sturdy and sustained opposition to the high-church outlook. The riot of styles evident in late nineteenth-century Nonconformist chapel-building did not unsettle these Strict Baptists. Few congregations could afford to follow such fashions, and the exceptions preferred something Classical, as at Bethesda, Ipswich. The Baptist leader C.H. Spurgeon, whose preference in such matters was well known, would have approved.

As was the case among the Independents, earlier chapels often had the pulpit set against one of the long walls and the front entrance(s) on the facing wall, so that none of the hearers were too far away from the preacher. At Grundisburgh, the best example in this book of such a plan, this made for a long gallery facing the pulpit. Other hipped-roof chapels were built to a square plan (making the roof pyramidal), such as Salhouse and Shelfanger. Some achieve real distinctiveness of ground plan and appearance, such as the two hexagonal (not coffin-shaped) chapels at Fressingfield and Friston, the outcome of one man's attempt to produce an economical preaching-box; we may parallel this with John Wesley's endorsement of octagonal chapels as eminently suitable for preaching in. After 1845, hipped-roof chapels ceased to be built and gabled ends took over; this reflected a trend to turn the interior through ninety degrees so that the pulpit was on a short wall, facing orderly rows of pews instead of the agglomeration of squarish box pews installed in earlier buildings.

Inside, the chapels of the earlier decades are light and airy, far from oppressive and certainly not mean (although the expense of erecting a building often took decades to pay off). Galleries are frequent, sometimes with shutters to permit their use by the Sunday School. Baptisms were initially conducted out of doors, some chapels having their own baptizing pond (e.g. Carleton Rode), but by the late nineteenth century comfort and a desire not to appear disrespectable or subject the ordinance to disrespect motivated most chapels to install baptisteries under the floors of their chapels, usually in front of the pulpit. Pews were provided downstairs, and sometimes upstairs too, but even where these instead of plain benches were used in the galleries, the quality of finish was not always as high; doubtless the pew rents were lower too! Singers' pews such as are found in some contemporary Methodist chapels are unusual, and if they survive they are usually located in the gallery by the organ rather than near the pulpit (e.g. Laxfield); choirs rarely achieved the prominence in Strict Baptist chapels (in Suffolk or Norfolk, at least) that they did in other denominations. In front of the pulpit would be the communion table, perhaps inscribed with a biblical text such as 'This do in remembrance of me', with seats for the pastor flanked by his deacons. At the doors offertory boxes were often mounted, sometimes with suitable texts enjoining giving by the Lord's people. The churches in this book were slow to adopt such money-raising devices as bazaars, and very seldom put on entertainments. Subscriptions from members, however, were more acceptable, and represented their attempt to practice the principle of systematic giving to God's work.

And what about the names? Biblical ones predominated. In these counties the most popular were Zion (8) and Providence (7). Some imply things about the congregation's history, such as Rehoboth (4; see Bury St Edmunds) or Cave Adullam (3; see Ipswich, Mount Zion). Unlike the Methodists, there are no Brunswicks, Hanovers or Victorias – but we do have a Martyrs' Memorial.

The Twentieth Century

A few twentieth-century buildings appear in this book: Bethesda, Ipswich (1913); Aldringham (1915); Zoar, Ipswich (1925); Leiston, Faith (1927); Whitton, Ipswich (1952); Kesgrave (1968); Bradfield and Rougham (1980); Cransford (1990); and Shepherd Drive, Ipswich (1995). Most may be said to continue the vernacular tradition, demonstrating characteristics of other buildings from their period, but those at Aldringham, Bethesda and Zoar stand out.

As for the churches, by 1904 growth had slowed, and the moderator of the Suffolk and Norfolk Association (W.F. Edgerton of Rattlesden) was asking why Strict Baptists were not growing as other Baptists were. His reasons included rural depopulation, competition from hard-working high-church Anglican clergy, the arrival of other denominations, the lack of pastors, the low educational attainments of village chapel memberships, the lack of evangelistic spirit, and the evil of drink. He called for greater exertion in work among children and overseas mission support, and asserted that there were some churches which ought to join the association. Many of these notes have continued to be sounded. In particular, Strict Baptists seem to have found it difficult to shake off a sense of inferiority, making references to it, and to perceptions of them as anachronistic, at various points. Some, however, were confident of the continuing need for a Strict Baptist witness: in 1927 it was recorded that Abner Morling, a much loved Suffolk pastor who died that year, had insisted on this, because 'We keep them others right.'[9] Religious revival came to various parts of Britain in 1904, 1921 (affecting Lowestoft and Yarmouth) and 1949; but there was little impact on local Strict Baptists.

By contrast, World War I had a terrific impact on the churches. By mid 1915 no less than forty men from the congregation at Tunstall had gone to serve in the armed forces, and that before conscription became compulsory. Apart from the losses to which memorial tablets in a number of chapels bear witness, the social dislocation resulting from the war meant that village society would never be the same again. Moreover, improving transport and increased leisure time all brought new challenges and alternatives to attendance at chapel. When war broke out again in 1939, men were again called up, but this time fewer were killed. This time, however, the buildings were affected much more than had been the case before. Several were requisitioned for government or military use, and a number were damaged by enemy action, including Friston, Great Yarmouth, Norwich (Orford Hill), Stonham and Waldringfield. Blackouts severely curtailed evening activities, and the association meetings were replaced by regional gatherings to lessen the use of scarce petrol rations.

The Sunday School at Great Blakenham during the early twentieth century (courtesy of the AGBC(EA))

---

[9] *Circular Letter on 'The Church's Attitude to the World's Pleasures and Problems,'* by the Suffolk and Norfolk Association of Particular Baptist Churches ... (Ipswich, 1927), p.10.

A greater emphasis was now being placed on children's work. From time to time it was found necessary to stress that a Sunday School was not an independent republic but an integral part of the local congregation's outreach. Its anniversary remained a highlight of the congregation's year, alongside Harvest Thanksgiving and the anniversaries of the pastor and the church, but some churches were lamenting the decline in numbers of children attending Sunday worship. Others, however, were beginning midweek meetings for them. A few of the town churches introduced Girls' or Boys' Brigades. In 1928 the Sunday School Branch of the association came into being, primarily in response to concern felt at the decline in Sunday School attendance, and until recently its annual rally rounded off the second day of the tent meetings.

The formation of the Sunday School Branch was one example of a trend towards centralization observable in various quarters during the 1920s and 1930s. At the national level, the Fellowship of Youth was formed in 1934, the National Strict Baptist Sunday School Association about the same time, and the National Federation of Strict Baptist Churches in 1946. In Suffolk, an evangelistic committee (the Village Mission) was formed in 1931, which overlapped with the Home Missionary Society, and the two did not join forces until 1960. Gospel Standard churches saw the appearance of the 'God Honouring Movement' in 1934, which sought to establish a clear demarcation between Gospel Standard churches and other Strict Baptists.

The inter-war period saw the rise of mission services, series of meetings conducted in a church by a pastor from another church in the denomination. Whilst such services proved popular, their impact was probably fairly minimal, apart from those who were already fringe attenders. An association evangelist was appointed from 1923–6, 1956–61 and 1979–84 (most of the men so appointed combined this with a part-time pastorate), but the main evangelistic impact has been from the work of the local congregation itself. Other groups could provide specialist evangelistic ministry, and the decline of tent missions meant change in the nature of evangelistic events.

After World War II there was a surge of outreach. New village stations were opened, and a tent purchased by the association in 1948 for evangelistic campaigns. But by the end of the 1960s almost all the village stations had gone; none now remain. For many chapels, decline in membership means that resources are concentrated on activities at the main centre, while for larger causes evangelism now takes forms radically different from those of earlier years. However, a number maintain regular services in accommodation for elderly people or engage in literature distribution. Outreach activities now often focus on making contact with unchurched people, the need for such activities perhaps indicating how social interaction generally has declined in modern society. One new venture was summer beach missions, the first being held at Hunstanton in 1976. These sought to reach adults as well as children. Apart from those converted through this work, young people have found the missions an invaluable training ground. Locally, by 1994 most churches in the association were holding children's holiday clubs or missions every year or two. Meetings for women have also continued to be a major feature of the outreach of most chapels; more recently, the men have begun to receive attention, with golf and football being among the activities on offer. Most chapels have adapted their premises to take account of new patterns of outreach and worship, new requirements, and higher expectations of comfort. Pews were often replaced by upholstered chairs. Schoolrooms have been added where these did not exist before, and kitchen and toilet facilities installed.

In the early 1950s the association numbered 40 churches; now it comprises 28; membership has declined from around 2,000 to 1,100, almost half of which can be attributed to the withdrawal of the large church at Bethesda, Ipswich. Sunday schools had about 2,500 children on their books until the late 1950s, since when these have declined sharply, the decline being only partly offset by the trend to replace Sunday Schools by weeknight activities (now declining in their turn). Baptisms reported reached a post-war peak of 116 in 1985, perhaps in the wake of the Billy Graham 'Mission England', but have also fallen in more recent years.

Sadly, many chapels have closed, often being converted to private dwellings and rarely retaining much external evidence of their previous function. Others have left Strict Baptist circles, often because of the communion issue. During the earlier part of the twentieth century some joined the Baptist Union; more recently, such churches have found fellowship with other independent evangelical congregations. But a few new buildings have been opened during the century. One new opening which has not been exploited as much as had been hoped concerns the post-war housing estates which have mushroomed on the edge of most of the area's towns. Bury, Haverhill, Ipswich and Lowestoft all saw large-scale development, as did Norwich. In 1965 a Vision and Venture Fund was launched to raise £50,000 in seven years to purchase sites for new work. But the only new site to be developed so far has been on the Chantry estate, south of the centre of Ipswich, where Shepherd Drive Baptist Church was opened in 1995. There have also been attempts to establish a work in Bury St Edmunds: a children's work was supported briefly around 1970, and more recently the Bradfield and Rougham church has established a satellite congregation on the large Moreton Hall estate.

Strict Baptists in the Area Today

The association has experienced fluctuating fortunes as churches have either expressed a heightened sense of denominational identity or adopted a more independent and self-sufficient approach to congregational life. Some only joined it when they were dying, such as Bury St Edmunds, Wortwell or Great Yarmouth. Others have felt able to withdraw from participation and often also from membership. Heartfelt pleas have continued to be made by smaller churches for participation and support from their larger sisters, and not infrequently one church has come to the aid of another, providing regular preachers, helping to keep outreach activities going and so on. Interdependence and independence are two easily confused concepts, and debate about which is preferable is unlikely soon to reach a final resolution. Some churches which are not themselves members nevertheless link up with the children's work of the association.

During the last three decades there has been a noticeable increase in the number of people transferring in and out of the churches in the association, in line with the increase in social mobility generally. This has meant that many have joined the churches who are unfamiliar with Strict Baptist distinctive beliefs and practices, and these have come under some pressure as a result, most notably the restriction of participation in communion to those baptized by immersion as believers. Pastors, too, have come and gone, and the proportion of those with deep roots in Suffolk and Norfolk has declined markedly, a fact which has implications for the ability of the association as a whole to remain suitably 'inculturated', in rural areas at least.

Of course, Suffolk and Norfolk are no longer as far from the beaten track as they were; the London commuter zone reaches to Norwich, and main roads see increasing freight traffic to and from mainland Europe. For many reasons, the associated Strict Baptists of this area are now much less distinctive than they used to be when compared to other Strict Baptists and to other conservatively minded evangelicals. Their story is less easy to separate out than it was; but it remains worth telling, and the churches are vigorous enough for an onlooker to expect that they have plenty of future.

NORFOLK

■ = open; □ = closed; + = mission station / branch church; Gospel Standard causes are ringed

- Tips End
- King's Lynn
- Downham Market
- Southery
- Swaffham
- Martham
- Gt Yarmouth
- Norton Subcourse
- Haddiscoe
- Toft Monks
- Gillingham
- Burgh St Peter
- Geldeston
- Aylsham
- Blofield
- Claxton
- Loddon
- Hales
- Salhouse
- Norwich
- Mulbarton
- Framingham Pigot
- Brooke
- Saxlingham Thorpe
- Bunwell
- Hempnall
- North Green
- Pulham
- Harleston
- Wortwell
- Needham
- Brockdish
- Deopham
- Gt Ellingham
- Attleborough
- Carleton Rode
- Old Buckenham
- Banham
- Kenninghall
- Tivetshall
- Shelfanger
- Burston
- Rushall
- Billingford
- E Harling
- Fersfield
- S Lopham
- Bressingham

SUFFOLK

1. Ashbocking
2. Barham
3. Beyton
4. Blaxhall
5. Brandeston
6. Brockford
7. Buxhall
8. Claydon
9. Cotton
10. Crowfield
11. Drinkstone
12. Earl Soham
13. Earl Stonham
14. Foxhall
15. Framlingham
16. Framsden
17. Hacheston
18. Hacheston
19. Hawstead
20. Hessett
21. Kesgrave
22. Knodishall
23. Martlesham
24. Mettingham
25. Occold
26. Parham
27. Playford
28. Ringsfield
29. Ringshall
30. Rougham
31. Saxmundham
32. Somersham
33. Stoke Ash
34. Swilland
35. Waldringfield
36. Witnesham
37. Woodbridge
38. Worlingham
39. Wyverstone

Attleborough

In 1820 the Norfolk and Suffolk Association reported the dismissal of 18 members from Diss to form a church at Attleborough. Later accounts, however, state that the church was formed from Great Ellingham and Kenninghall after a disagreement at Ellingham. Whichever is the case, services began in 1819 in a home, later moving to a barn. A chapel was built in 1832 which could seat 500 people. The story goes that one night the pastor at the time, Joseph Green, moved the stakes marking out where the walls were to go, making the building larger than had been intended.

The church never joined any Strict Baptist association, but was identified as Strict Baptist in the 1851 Religious Census, when it reported attendances of 200 in the morning, 350 in the afternoon, and 100 in the evening. During the mid nineteenth century it was also part of a small grouping known as the Friendly Union, which included the nearby churches of Carleton Rode, Kenninghall and Shelfanger. However, the church has long been a member of the Norfolk Association and its successor, the Eastern Baptist Association. During the mid twentieth century it was pastored jointly with the churches at Great Ellingham and, for some of the time, Wymondham.

A burial ground was added in 1856, but this was the cause of dissension and the formation of an independent church at Old Buckenham, which had been a branch work. The first chapel was demolished in 1960, although the old gravestones remain. The replacement building shown in the picture was opened in 1979.

Location: Leys La, NR17 2HX; OS grid ref.: TM045949

Brooke

Work in this locality began with cottage meetings in nearby Kirstead. The chapel appears to have been built in 1841, reusing materials from another building in Kirstead (hence the date '1831' on two shields in the door frame): in 1839 G.S. Kett of Brooke Hall had offered a chapel on his land to the Norfolk & Norwich Association, but negotiations fell through because of his insistence that the church should practise open communion. The chapel was, however, re-erected in Brooke and the cause continued, but it is not known how it came to adopt a strict communion position.

The chapel's external appearance, which includes a stepped gable and Tudor detailing, is unique among the buildings in this book. The cause reached a low point during the 1920s. It was on the Gospel Standard list from the 1930s, but more recently it has developed closer links with some of the Grace Baptist churches, particularly that at Fressingfield.

Location: 50 High Green, NR15 1JA; NR OS grid ref.: TM 281987

For further information

H. Hoadley, *A History of Brooke Strict Baptist Chapel, nr. Norwich, Norfolk, Compiled from the Fragments that Remain*, n.pl., 1964

Carleton Rode*

A congregation had been meeting in the village since 1774 as a branch of that at Great Ellingham. The chapel was built in 1811 on land given by one John Barnard, who also paid for the building, and a church formed the following year by the dismissal of members from Diss.

Like the chapel at Stowmarket, its solid appearance belies the fact that it lacks foundations. An unusual survival is the baptizing pond by the roadside behind the chapel. Until interior baptisteries were built, churches without a nearby stream for baptizing would have had such ponds.

In 1854 the church withdrew from the Friendly Union because it wished to maintain strict communion, on which it disagreed with the church at Great Ellingham, which that year adopted an open table. The church was briefly in membership with the Suffolk and Norfolk Association during the early 1860s, probably at the wish of its new pastor, James Kerridge from the Friston church. When he left, the church left the association. It adopted open communion in 1925, having joined the Baptist Union earlier in the century.

Stabling for horses was provided in the 1860s and facilities for the Sunday School above this in 1904. In 2012 a coffee shop was opened, using the parking area underneath the school rooms.

Location: 6 Chapel Rd, NR16 1RN; OS grid ref.: TM 118930

For further information

A. Bancroft, *Carleton Rode Baptist Church Ter-Jubilee 1812–1962*, Norwich, 1962

Records

NRO: FC46/1–4 (microfilms MF1619/8–9 etc), church books 1811–1933, minutes 1895–1947, birth & death register 1801–37

The baptizing pond, complete with warning sign

Claxton

The chapel before the 1993 fire (Ken Hipper)

Standing above the fields on a back lane in the middle of nowhere is one of the most atmospheric of the Norfolk chapels featured in this book. A Particular Baptist congregation was formed in Claxton around 1750, when the remnants of a congregation at Beccles were brought together by Henry Utting, a local farmer who served as the church's pastor from 1765 to 1792. He hosted them in his house, and later paid most of the cost of a new meeting house, which was registered in 1765 although the now-destroyed deeds indicate that it was apparently built a decade or more earlier. The original west wall (which may initially have formed the front wall of the chapel) remains, against which a lean-to vestry was erected, apparently during the late eighteenth century.

The chapel appears to have been enlarged or rebuilt at some point in the 1790s (possibly with financial assistance from the Countess of Huntingdon), and almost completely rebuilt at some point in the mid nineteenth century, the floor area being increased and the walls heightened (as can be seen in the picture). The size of the congregation would have necessitated this: in 1851 it was reported as 500 in the morning and 600 in the evening. An old postcard on the 'Claxton Opera' website shows that the pulpit was located on the wall between the two doors, and since that wall has a bricked-up window opening we may conclude that when enlarged the chapel was also reorientated.

From 1794 to 1849, the pastor was Job Hupton, a former Countess of Huntingdon's Connexion preacher whose views on baptism had changed during his ministry at Dairy Lane, Ipswich. The church was in membership with the Suffolk and Norfolk Association from 1831 to 1838, but thereafter pursued an independent course, possibly of a more markedly high Calvinistic stamp. Even during those years, its membership was declining, from 140 to 112. In 1851 there was a day school in the vestry but no Sunday School.

Little is known of the church's later history. An organ was acquired in 1894 out of concern for the poor singing; one member is supposed to have commented that there was no more harm in a dead instrument than in dead singers. The last recorded church meeting was in 1930, and the cause was still in existence as late as 1931, the chapel apparently closing in 1943.

After post-closure use as a store, the chapel was converted into a dwelling – but not just an ordinary one: it includes a galleried room large enough to stage operatic productions, which take place each year under the designation 'Claxton Opera'. The owners had to cope with a devastating fire in 1993 but rapidly and lovingly restored the building. Outside, some of the original gravestones have been retained.

Location: Folly La; OS grid ref.: TG 336027

For further information

Anon., *Claxton: A Thousand Years of Village Life*, Claxton, 2005

'Claxton Opera', www.claxtonopera.co.uk

Downham Market, Zion

Very little is known of the work here. The chapel was built in 1849, but congregations in the 1851 census were not large, 35 in the morning and 45 in the afternoon. It was rebuilt 1874 and then seated 170 people, but Strict Baptist use had ceased by 1933. It was later the home of the Salvation Army corps, but when I saw it in 2007 they had moved and it appeared to be disused. Since then it has been converted and is now a florist's.

Location: 47 Priory Rd (B1512; formerly known as Parson's La), PE38 9UJ; OS grid ref.: TF 611031

Framingham Pigot

The church here was founded in 1808, and the chapel built the same year. As so often, it is located out of the village. It was in membership with the new association from 1831 to 1839. Membership in the late 1830s was 80, and in 1851 it reported average Sunday congregations of 50 in the mornings and 100 in the afternoons. The church was still active in 1867, but its history thereafter is largely unknown. The building was taken over from trustees by the church at Claxton in 1895, in an attempt to recommence work, and there is also a reference to its being reopened by the cause at Providence, Norwich, in 1902, but that is all we know.

Location: Chapel La; OS grid ref.: TG282037

Records

TNA: RG4/1136, births, 1808–36

Great Ellingham*

This church is the oldest to feature in this book, dating back to 1699. It is not clear how it originated, but it soon grew, and at some point appears to have erected a meeting house to replace the barn in which services had been held. Among those baptized here was the hymn-writer Robert Robinson, in 1759. Later in the century, the cause stagnated and the meeting house ceased to be used. Members met in a small cottage which still stands, to the right of the chapel.

At the end of the century, things looked up. A baptistery was added in 1799, and the chapel rethatched in 1802 (an indication that it was probably pretty similar in appearance to contemporary domestic and farm buildings).

The present chapel was built in 1824, and in 1847 a gallery was added. Average congregations in 1851 were reported as 170 in the mornings, 324 in the afternoons, and 140 in the evenings. A British School was established on church property in 1855, remaining there until new premises were provided for it in 1896. It appears that for part of the nineteenth century the church adopted hyper-Calvinistic views, this being one of the evils reportedly affecting the church around 1850 (reliance on endowment income was the other!). Yet just a few years later, in 1854, it adopted the practice of open communion. It had joined the Norfolk Baptist Association in 1847 and in 1896 it joined the Baptist Union.

When the building was restored in 1884 a new baptistery and porch were added, and the pulpit and pews were replaced. The tablet on the front gable was also added, but the date is that of the church's founding rather of the building itself. According to the church's website, 'Much of the cost was met by Jeremiah Colman (of Colman's Mustard fame) who attended the church and is commemorated on a brass plaque in the chapel.'

In 1895 part of the front wall was destroyed in a storm during the morning service, probably the same day as the Pulham St Mary chapel also sustained serious damage. In 1897, patriotic glass (red and blue) was placed in the windows either side of the pulpit, to mark the diamond jubilee of Queen Victoria.

From the 1960s the church gradually moved back to its earlier theological standpoint. It withdrew from the local association and the Baptist Union in 1971, for doctrinal reasons, and in 1975 returned to its original practice of strict communion, in line with its trust deed. It joined the Suffolk and Norfolk Association from 1981 to 1988, and although distance from other member churches had proved an obstacle to closer relationships it rejoined in 1995. Since then, it has prospered and extensions were completed to the left of the chapel in 1998, providing auxiliary accommodation.

Location: Long St, NR17 1LN; OS grid ref.: TM 019966

For further information

David Bugden, *'Still faithful to our God': The Story of 300 years of the Baptist Church at Great Ellingham*, Great Ellingham, 1999

www.gebc.org.uk

Records

NRO: FC56 (microfilm MF/RO425/5), records, 1699–1789

SBHS: church roll, 1701–89 (photocopy)

TNA: RG4/1254, burials, 1817–37

This picture of the interior shows the plain pews favoured during the late nineteenth century; the carved ends downstairs are worth noting.

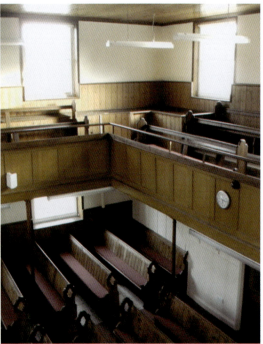

Great Yarmouth, Zoar / Salem

This cause began in 1841, when a group left the Particular Baptist church meeting at the Tabernacle. They met in a cottage, then in Zoar Chapel, Bank Paved Row. 'Zoar' means 'little', and according to the 1851 Religious Census return this building accommodated just 80 people (with a maximum congregation of 70 on the census day); it was not set apart for worship, and is likely to have been a room hired for services.

In 1853, therefore, the church opened Salem Chapel in Albion Rd. Twenty years later this was replaced by a chapel in Park Rd.

The church was in membership with the Suffolk and Norfolk Association from 1862 to 1879, by when membership had reached 34.

The congregation tended to rely on good numbers of summer visitors, and it is questionable whether it ever established a strong local membership base. The chapel certainly closed during both world wars, when visitors would have been few and far between. Damage during World War II meant that it did not reopen until 1949. It rejoined the Strict Baptist association on reopening, but by then had just five members. Closure came in 1966 and the building was used by an Elim Pentecostal church, but it has since been converted into flats.

Location: York Rd; OS grid ref.: TG528072

For further information

James Tann, 'New Baptist Chapel at Yarmouth', *EV* vol. 9 (1853), p.43

Records

AGBC(EA): minutes, 1922–51; Sunday School minutes, 1924–39; account books etc

Harleston

In 1820 a house in Chapel Yard was licensed for preaching by the newly formed church at Wortwell. In 1851 this was described as a chapel, seating 100 and with an evening congregation of 35. This could have been the former Independent chapel, which became surplus to requirements when they moved to a new one in 1819. It seems that until 1846 services may have been conducted alternately by Baptists and Independents, but after that date, when work was commenced by Pulham St Mary, the Baptists had it to themselves.

A reference in the Wortwell records to it as a 'sister church' indicates that by about 1860 it was more than a mission station, although it does not appear ever to have joined any of the Baptist associations. By 1879 it was once again under the care of the church at Pulham St Mary. Service were still being held here in 1892, but I have not come across any subsequent references. When I visited the location in 2012, the chapel appeared to have gone.

From 1982, the church at Fressingfield held regular services in the town for some years, but no church was formed.

Kenninghall*

Baptist outreach began in this village in the late 1790s, and a church was formed from Shelfanger in 1799. It met in a barn and then in a small chapel built for it (which does not appear to have survived). Services ceased in 1804 because, it was later recorded, of the lack of duly observed church order and discipline. However, after only a short interval another chapel was opened in 1807. It is unusual in being faced with flint, the only others in this book being at Barrow, Lakenheath and West Row, all in the far west of Suffolk. A church was formed in 1810 by the dismissal of 33 members from Diss. Galleries round three sides of the building were added in 1813 and a Sunday School in 1820.

Membership increased to over 130 by 1823, but division came in 1824. This appears to have been due to problems caused by the conduct of the pastor, Charles Box, who was denying members their customary privileges to speak in church meetings and otherwise acting arbitrarily. As a result, for a while there was a second chapel in the village, almost opposite the original, built in 1825. It was paid for by a schoolmaster, Thomas Humphrey. He put forward a plan for the interior arrangement but at a church meeting alleged that the membership had rejected this, and left the members to come up with their own; unanimously they adopted his! Pointedly, the chapel was named Bethezel (Micah 1.11; 'the neighbouring house'), the only instance of this name I have ever come across. Reunion was only possible once Box finally surrendered the church records to the legal trustees, enabling the new church (which had grown rapidly, whereas the congregation in the original chapel had shrunk to a handful) to return to the old building. This closed in 1830 upon reconciliation being achieved, and no trace of it appears to have remained, although it possessed a burial ground. Significantly, the church rules drawn up that year stipulated that in the event of any further division, the church records were to belong to that part of the congregation which was legally entitled to the meeting house.

The register of births kept until 1837 records 477 children, and gives the father's occupation. It is noticeable that apart from 3 children born to writers and 5 recorded as illegitimate, all were born to manual workers of some kind. Labourers accounted for 212 entries, 40 children were born to shoemakers, 31 to carpenters, 29 to farmers, and 24 to linen weavers. It shows the social and economic status of many of these rural congregations, and we may infer that they had few resources to fall back on when times were hard, as they often were for nineteenth-century agricultural communities. As a schoolmaster, Humphrey would therefore been looked to for leadership in the congregation.

Membership remained over a hundred for several decades, and the chapel was extended in 1832 and a schoolroom, vestries (1868) and porch (1874) added later. In 1851, congregations were reported as averaging 282 in the morning, 356 in the afternoon, and 130 in the evening; one wonders how such apparently precise figures were arrived at! However, by the end of the century the membership was down to the forties and, although the church rejoined the Suffolk and Norfolk Association in 1891 (possibly thinking this would help it in its search for a pastor), a long inexorable decline followed. Kenninghall had been parent to several congregations, among them Attleborough, Bardwell, Old Buckenham and South Lopham, and possibly also an early cause at East Harling, but by the 1920s it was reliant on the support of the Strict and Particular Baptist Society. In 1966 the Suffolk and Norfolk Association placed an evangelist in the village. Sadly, initial hopes for the work were not realized, and the chapel closed in 1971. Since then it has been a pottery and a museum, before becoming a private dwelling.

Location: Church St; OS grid ref.: TM040861

For further information

Gill and Peter Anderson, *The Story of the Kenninghall Baptists*, Kenninghall, 1989

Records

NRO: FC92/1-4 (microfilms MF1618/10, 1619/1-3), minutes, 1823-96; birth register, 1795-1837; burial register, 1818-84

King's Lynn, Zion

About 1832, a high Calvinist group left the Particular Baptist church meeting in Broad St. They built a small chapel in Blackfriars Rd, but it is not possible to date this with certainty: a reference in 1851 stated that they were seeking to provide a building, but that year's census return and another reference in 1857 indicated that the congregation had met at Zion Chapel since 1836; perhaps the first chapel was proving unsuitable. It is also unclear whether a church was actually formed here. Congregations in 1851 were certainly small: 30 in the morning and 16 in the evening, in a building seating 120. Around 1880 it was being supplied by Zoar, Norwich, indicating that it had adopted a Gospel Standard outlook. It closed by 1907, becoming a mission hall. By 1936 it was being used by a Spiritualist congregation; it has since been demolished.

For further information

W. Munday, 'The Cause of God and Truth at King's Lynn, Norfolk', *EV* vol. 7 (1851), p.48

R. Claydon, 'Lynn, Norfolk', *EV* vol. 13 (1857), p.118

Norwich, Gildencroft

Surprisingly, statistics indicated that in 1880 Norwich had more Strict Baptists than any other English cathedral city. However, their story is full of divisions and mergers, and has proved almost impossible to trace!

Built for the Quakers in the 1690s, this imposing meeting house came to be used primarily, though not exclusively, by Strict Baptists who formed a new church after the St Mary's Chapel case in 1860. This established the legal position that strict communion was not fundamental to Particular Baptist church order. It seems, however, that a schism had been in prospect for a couple of years. The decision to open up the communion service to all believers had been taken by St Mary's in 1857. Two trustees began a legal challenge in 1858, and the same year a group began meeting in a former warehouse in Magdalen St.

The Friends delayed in agreeing to let the meeting house until about 1860. Imposing though it was, it was evidently not all that the Strict Baptists could desire:

> We deeply feel that the situation of our chapel is in the way of our prosperity. We have not only to contend against the strong current of popular opinion in the professedly Christian church, whereby we are unrighteously judged to be *narrow, exclusive* and *bigoted*; but we have also to contend against *narrow, dirty,* and *exclusive lanes,* and *alleys,* leading to the chapel, up which in dark and unpleasant weather many persons object to come.[1]

Still, they were allowed to install a baptistery in 1868/9, unusually above rather than below floor level. In 1879 a formerly Brethren congregation merged with them, which may explain why the church withdrew from the Suffolk and Norfolk Association in 1880 and two years later joined the Norfolk and Norwich Association. By this point it had about a hundred members. Decline ensued; late in the century, it is said that a group from the church emigrated to Australia. Around 1893 the interior was converted for the use of an adult school, which implies that the Baptists were not prospering. In 1915 the church was dissolved, and (ironically) Baptist work came under the oversight of St Mary's. Services ceased in 1939. The building was largely destroyed by bombing in 1942, and although rebuilt in 1958 it burnt down in 1990.

For further information

David Butler, *The Quaker Meeting Houses of Britain* (2 vols, London, 1999), vol. 1, pp.454-5, with drawing

Lucy Parker, 'Gildencroft Meeting House and Burial Ground', www.heritagecity.org/research-centre/churches-and-creeds/gildencroft-meeting-house-and-burial-ground.htm

---

[1] *Circular Letter on the Glory of Christ: by the Suffolk and Norfolk Association of Particular Baptist Churches, met in Grundisburgh* … (Beccles, 1865), p.31.

Norwich, Jireh

This cause began independently of Orford Hill and belonged to a different strand of Strict Baptists. The congregation first met in a room in Bedford St, known as the 'Hole in the Wall', during the late 1830s. It migrated to Jireh Chapel in Dereham Rd, which was opened by William Gadsby in 1840. Apart from being (I think) then only time he preached in Norfolk or Suffolk, this was, apparently, the only time when he 'begged' for a congregation to give generously to a cause. 'Jireh' comes from Genesis 22, in which Abraham assures his son Isaac, whom he has been commanded to sacrifice, that God will provide the lamb for the burnt offering – and he does, Isaac being released just in time. The name was often used for a chapel in order to express faith in, and thanksgiving for, God's provision of a place of worship.

When Jireh's pastor, George Muskett, moved on in 1849, the congregation dispersed, some to Providence or Orford Hill and others (presumably those who were most strongly Gadsbyite in their thinking, who would not have been happy with the ministry in the other chapels) meeting in a local synagogue. Muskett attempted to reopen the chapel in 1865 but his health soon failed and the chapel closed again, this time being converted into two houses. These remained standing until after World War II but I have been unable to trace them.

What was left of the congregation met for a few years in a room in Pottergate St which had been formerly used by the Wesleyans, before merging with Providence around 1870.

Norwich, Orford Hill*

The building about 1990; two of the entrances have been closed up (Ken Hipper)

This cause may have begun as the result of division at St Mary's Baptist Church when a new minister, William Brock, arrived in 1832. Joseph Kinghorn, the minister since 1789, had adopted closed communion views during the 1790s, providing a lead to Baptists locally and nationally. With his death, a change of outlook was soon evident.

In 1833 the church took over a late eighteenth-century warehouse. As converted it had three front entrances and seated 500. In the 1851 census, attendance was 420 in the morning, 150 in the afternoon and 450 in the evening.

In 1862 the church stood aloof from the Norfolk and Norwich Association because it could not practise intercommunion with open-communion churches. The following year William Brown, the pastor, moved to Fressingfield, apparently taking the church books with him! The church joined the Suffolk and Norfolk Association in 1868, remaining a member until closure.

A new schoolroom was added in 1900, and when the chapel was severely damaged during an air raid in 1942, the congregation had to meet in the schoolroom until repairs were completed in 1950. Although membership rose to 163 in 1889, the annual reports to the association give the impression of a church which was weaker than statistics might imply. By 1947 the membership had plummeted to 9. Closure followed in 1975, formally a merger of the congregation with that at Salhouse, thus reversing the arrangement by which Salhouse had been for some years a mission of Orford Hill. The building was converted once more, and is now a restaurant.

Location: Orford Hill, NR1 3LA; OS grid ref.: TG231083

Records

SBHS: minutes, 1857–1975; membership roll, 1858–1911

A plaque on the wall offers an unusual if inaccurate variation on Baptist denominational names.

Norwich, Providence

Built in 1769 for the Calvinistic Methodists, Providence Chapel was hired in 1814 by friends of Abraham Pye, who had been the pastor at Saxlingham. When Pye refused to share the pulpit with another man, he left and rented the former French church in Queen St (later used by the Catholic Apostolic Church). The Pitt St chapel was purchased by the Particular Baptists in 1818 and Pye returned. Access to it was through a doorway between 33 and 35 Pitt St. In 1851 congregations here were 139 in the morning, 99 in the afternoon, and 110 in the evening, in a building seating 300. This congregation seems to have been active as late as 1875 but then disappears.

From 1879 to 1886 the chapel was used by the Gospel Standard congregation which moved to Zoar. It was reopened once more, in 1898, for a group which broke away from Orford Hill. They too appear to have had Gospel Standard leanings, as they linked up with the 'God Honouring Movement' in 1934, which called on doctrinal grounds for a complete separation from preachers and churches not listed in the *Gospel Standard*. In the same year they merged with Zoar and vacated Providence, as the latter was structurally unsound and also due for demolition under a scheme to build a new road.

A photograph in the Zoar history, *Thou shalt remember*, shows the cottages in front of the chapel as they stood in 1936; demolition of the cottages and the chapel followed soon afterwards.

For further information

Anon., *A Declaration of the Faith and Practice of the Church of Christ, at Providence Chapel, Norwich, under the pastoral care of Abraham Pye, read and assented to at the admission of members*, Norwich, 1864

www.georgeplunkett.co.uk/Norwich/old.htm#Pitts

Norwich, Zoar

Zoar Strict Baptist Chapel is within 50 metres of the Norwich Central Baptist Church, but its origins are entirely separate. About 1871, the union of Providence with a remnant from Jireh resulted in a schism. In 1875, this group hired the Tabernacle, St Martin-at-Palace Plain, which had been opened in 1755 and soon afterwards sold to the Countess of Huntingdon for her Connexion: this was a chain of chapels maintained at the noble lady's expense and employing evangelical chaplains whom she regarded as ministers of the Church of England. A church was formed the same year, and the congregation moved in 1879 to Providence Chapel. After serving as a garage and a timber store, the Tabernacle was demolished in 1953; there is a picture of it in the Zoar history, *Thou shalt remember*.

From Providence, the church moved in 1886 to a new chapel, Zoar. The name is significant, Zoar being the 'little' place of refuge to which Lot fled before Sodom and Gomorrah were destroyed (Genesis 19.20-22), a contrast from the thousand-seater Providence. The cause has always been associated with the Gospel Standard churches. By the late nineteenth century, Zoar was supplying preaching at Aylsham, Blofield, Ho(r)ning, Mulbarton and even Kings Lynn and Downham Market, over forty miles away. A short-lived schism in 1900 produced a congregation which met in the Gordon Hall, Duke St, but this petered out after a few years. Remarkably, when most buildings around it were destroyed by bombing in 1942, including St Mary's Baptist Church, Zoar remained standing. It continues today, the last survivor of Norwich's Strict Baptist congregations.

Location: St Mary's Plain, NR3 3AF; OS grid ref.: TG228091

For further information

[William Fay], *Thou shalt remember … : A Short History of the Strict and Particular Baptist Church meeting at Zoar, St Mary's Plain, Norwich*, Norwich, 1948

Records

NRO: FC110, deeds relating to the site, 1744-1886

Old Buckenham*

Preaching in the village was carried out from the church at Attleborough during the 1820s. A branch church was formed in 1825 by the dismissal of members from Attleborough, and a chapel was provided in 1831/2 by a Mr Norton. From 1830 to 1851 it seems to have shared a minister with Great Ellingham, although the latter was an independent work. From 1855 until 1859, when it became independent, Old Buckenham came under the oversight of the church at Diss. The change seems to have been precipitated by the Attleborough church's expectation that Old Buckenham members would be willing to contribute to the cost of its new burial ground, which they were not. The change of oversight seems to have been a catalyst for renewed activity, as a new chapel was built in 1857.

Although described as Strict Baptist in the 1851 Religious Census, it never belonged to any Strict Baptist body, although it was part of the Friendly Union. In time it became part of the Norfolk Association. A Sunday School building was added to the rear of the chapel in 1887. In 1959 one entrance was made in the middle of the frontage, replacing two gabled porches. However, services ceased in 1991 and about 2007 the chapel was converted to a dwelling.

Location: Abbey Rd; OS grid ref.: TM066917

Records

NRO: FC108/1, plan of graveyard and chapel with list of monumental inscriptions, 1871–1971

NRO: FC 127/1-2 (microfilm MF1775/605-751, 1776/1-225), church minutes, 1856–1902, 1915–91; registers of members, 1856–1982; register of burials, 1858–97; deacons' minutes, 1915–44

Pulham St Mary

There had been a Baptist congregation in this village from the 1640s until well into the eighteenth century, and preaching from the Wortwell church in 1820, but nothing appears to have remained from these efforts. Meetings here were held in a cottage and then a barn before the chapel was opened in 1843. A church was formed in 1841, which remained in the Suffolk and Norfolk Association throughout its life; congregations increased to around three hundred and a gallery was added for the Sunday School in 1868, while membership rose to 92 in 1871. After the long ministry of Benjamin Taylor (1842–86), the church divided from 1887 to 1892. Reconciliation and re-formation came in the latter year, through the efforts of representatives of the association, but membership was only half what it had been before division. The chapel had to be rebuilt in 1895 after the end wall blew in during a storm on the morning of Sunday, 24 March, killing the pastor in the pulpit.

The church ceased to exist about 1952, but the burial ground remained in association hands as late as 1981. The chapel is now in industrial use.

Location: Station Rd, South Green; OS grid ref.: TM206843

Salhouse: Zion, Rehoboth and the Horseshoe Chapel

Zion Chapel (above) was built in 1802 for a church formed the previous year, and appears to have been altered in 1813 and largely rebuilt on safety grounds in 1828. As at Old Buckenham, a central entrance has replaced two doors either side.

The date '1813' on these bricks in the front wall suggests that this was when the frontage was altered.

In 1847, the home mission of the Norfolk and Norwich Association was overseeing a church here, though it is not clear which. It could have been that meeting at Rehoboth, in Upper St, converted as a place of worship in 1846 for a group which withdrew from Zion, possibly in 1841 (although this date is hard to square with other information); this congregation was still active in 1864 and possibly until well into the twentieth century. By 1851 Rehoboth was being led by the minister at Zion from 1844, Samuel Sergeant. In the 1851 Religious Census, Zion reported a total morning attendance of 124 and Rehoboth attendances of 80 in the morning, 140 in the afternoon, and 25 in the evening.

Sergeant subsequently became a Gospel Standard minister and was to be involved with a third cause in Salhouse. This was the Horseshoe Chapel, in the lane of that name. It is not clear whether the

Horseshoe Chapel is to be identified with the Particular Baptist chapel reporting a morning attendance of 142 in 1851, but a church appears to have been formed there, possibly by Sergeant, in 1853. Its subsequent history is unknown; although there were three Particular Baptist returns in the 1851 Religious Census, commercial directories stated that there were just two Baptist chapels in the village. At any rate, three Baptist congregations in a village with a population in 1851 of just 691 was quite remarkable. The Horseshoe Chapel was converted into two cottages during the inter-war period, in the face of local opposition, although its burial ground was still extant in 1948. As late as 1976 reference was being made to the former Strict Baptist chapel in Horseshoe Lane, implying that the building may still have been standing at that point.

By 1960 Zion was functioning as a mission of Norwich, Orford Hill; this was itself weak, and in 1975 activities were concentrated at Salhouse. After input from the Home Mission, and five years' support from Fressingfield and elsewhere, it ceased to be supported by the Strict Baptist association in 1986. However, efforts were immediately made to re-establish a worshipping congregation and the chapel remains open as the home of an independent Reformed Baptist church.

Location: Zion, Chapel Loke, NR13 6RA; OS grid ref.: TG314148

In 1847 the members of Zion purchased a former Methodist chapel in **Blofield**, and work continued there until about 1890. About 1880 Zoar, Norwich, was supplying preachers there, so by then it was presumably Gospel Standard. The property was sold in 1895, presented to the village in 1897 as a Reading Room, and now serves as the local library.

Location: North St, NR13 4RQ; OS grid ref.: TG334096

For further information

Anon., 'A New Beginning at Salhouse', G June 1986, p.15

David Bugden, 'Church Profile: Salhouse Baptist Church', G August/September 1992, pp.17–18

www.salhousebaptistchurch.com

Records

TNA: RG4/2046, births, 1802–37

Saxlingham Thorpe

Ken Hipper

Little is known of this church, which was formed in 1802 from St Mary's, Norwich (its minister, Joseph Kinghorn, was preaching there each month by 1799), although its first pastor was Abraham Pye (1803–14), who later took charge of Providence, Norwich. He preached in the village for two years before a church was formed. It was in membership with the Suffolk and Norfolk Association from 1847 to 1852, and later appeared in the list of churches put out by the *Christian's Pathway*., a magazine which catered to a viewpoint somewhere between that of the association and the Gospel Standard churches. My impression is that several churches in south Norfolk and the Waveney valley shared this outlook.

The chapel was opened in 1821, and in 1851 it reported congregations of 150 in the morning, 300 in the afternoon, and 200 in the evening, in a building claimed to seat 300. Membership in 1852 was 63. As with several Norfolk causes, little is known of its later history. The chapel finally closed in 1947, being converted to a dwelling.

Location: Windy La; OS grid ref.: TM216978

Records

TNA: RG4/1137, births, 1812–36

Shelfanger*

The pictures show the improvement which can be achieved by sensitive restoration of a chapel exterior (left-hand illustration: Ken Hipper)

This church was founded in 1765 by members of a Baptist church then extant at Beccles, among others. It met first of all in the village of Rushall before migrating to Shelfanger, an illustration of the wide catchment areas drawn on by many dissenting congregations during the seventeenth and eighteenth centuries before they began to multiply. Three years later a building, possibly a converted barn, at Shelfanger was opened for worship. When the chapel was (re)built in 1821 it retained a wooden-framed south-east side wall.

It was at the opening of the chapel in 1768 that the idea of an association of Particular Baptist churches was first mooted, arising from the circumstance that most Particular Baptist ministers in Norfolk and Suffolk were present to take part in the services and so had the opportunity to form acquaintance with one another. In 1769, the induction of the church's first pastor, Thomas Smith, provided the occasion for definite plans to be made and set in motion, and a further meeting took place later that year at Wattisham.

The young church appears to have encountered difficulties. The association's circular letter of 1779 says that the messengers assembled for the annual meetings considered its 'languid case', examining its neglect of the gospel ordinances (believer's baptism and the Lord's Supper) and advising the church to restore them. Nevertheless, Smith (who ministered from 1769 to 1813) saw several men sent out from the church into ministry in nearby congregations. He also wrote 1100 hymns for the use of his congregation, a practice which was not uncommon among Baptists and Independents from the late seventeenth century onwards, until the rise of the modern denominational hymnbook.

Side galleries were added to the chapel in 1835 and a Sunday School commenced, but a schism occurred in 1838. Although it did not last too long, the church's previous prosperity never returned, even though afternoon congregations in 1851 were around three hundred. An application to join the Suffolk and Norfolk Association in 1882 was postponed, and the following year declined. In the event the church never did join, although it sought advice from the association in 1923 and the officers were due to visit it in connection with yet another application for membership (which followed the death in 1922 of the man who since 1892 had been pastor). This was twice deferred, and the church was now quite weak. Regular church meetings ceased in 1927, as did the Sunday School after an outbreak of (unspecified) infectious disease. By 1929, Sunday afternoon services were being maintained with preachers coming mostly from Horham. There were no records of any kind kept after 1940.

A branch work was active at **Bressingham** by 1859, when a chapel was opened, confusingly also in Common Rd (but now no longer in existence). From 1881 it was being worked by the Baptist church at Diss, who had stepped in to help but by the mid 1920s were refusing to pay rent demanded by Shelfanger. When Diss ceased holding services in 1932, Shelfanger reopened the chapel. Services were still being held there as late as 1942, although by now both the mission and the parent church were weak.

Shelfanger itself did not close until 1968; sadly, appeals by the trustees for workers to recommence outreach here and at Kenninghall brought no response. The building was used as a workshop before being converted into a dwelling.

Location: Common Rd; OS grid ref.: TM106840

For further information

Maurice F. Hewett, 'The Church at Shelfanger', *Baptist Quarterly* vol. 12, no. 9 (January 1948), pp.331–40

G January 1971, p.8

GH vol. 50 (1882), pp.222–3

Records

SBHS: church books, 1765–1814, 1834–1940; membership lists, 1765–1825, 1834–77, 1880–1920; register of births, 1758–1824; register of marriages, 1904–20

TNA: RG4/1138, births, 1814–37

South Lopham

A mission was established here about 1850, away from the centre of the village, by the Kenninghall church, and this chapel was registered in 1851. The cause was recognized as an independent church in 1857, but was reportedly broken up by 1876, never having joined any association. In 1885 the work was being looked after from Shelfanger, but the chapel must have closed subsequently, because in 1892 it was reported as reopened. In 1899 the chapel was reopened by Shelfanger again, but was soon handed over to Kenninghall.

By 1901 there was a Sunday congregation of 60, but the work caused some problems for its parent, its attenders wishing to hold a communion service on mornings when no preacher was provided. This indicates possible Brethren influence, confirmed by subsequent events. Kenninghall were advised by the Suffolk and Norfolk Association in 1902 that this cause should not become independent, but it became a branch church in 1903. By 1912, however, a Brethren assembly was meeting here. This ceased to exist during the early 1990s. The chapel is now a private house but retains the burial ground.

Location: Low Common; OS grid ref.: TM058807

Southery

I have not established how this cause came into existence, but it is one of several Gospel Standard churches strung out along the edge of the Fens, and may owe something to the work of William Huntington and his followers. The ground to the front of the chapel looks as if it once held a larger building, but in fact the present tiny chapel or preaching room (seating 60 in 1851) is the original. It was built about 1845, although a church was not formed until 1900. At some point it lapsed, although services appear to have continued, and it was re-formed in 2001.

Location: Churchgate St, PE38 0ND; OS grid ref.: TL622946

Tips End, Zion

A Strict Baptist work was going on in the hamlet of Tips End, part of the parish of Welney in the south-western tip of Norfolk, by 1845, when a chapel was apparently built. The founder was one John Rowell, who died about 1850. It is not known where the first chapel was located, but a replacement was built in 1874 to a design by J. Kerridge. Although the chapel is located in the Norfolk half of Tips End, which straddles the border with Cambridgeshire, the church actually joined the Cambridgeshire and East Midlands Union of Strict Baptist Churches, formed in 1928. In latter years it was looked after by the Strict Baptist church at March.

The cause became famous for the annual strawberry tea, served on the occasion of the chapel anniversary. However, there was little settlement nearby, and around 1983 the chapel closed. It was de-registered as a place of worship in 2000, and is now a private dwelling.

Location: Lakesend Rd (off B1100); OS grid ref.: TL509951

Wortwell, Providence

In 1818, disaffected Baptist members of the Independent church at Denton asked William Ward, Baptist minister at Diss, to provide them a preacher. A 'preaching house' was opened in 1819, and later that year 18 members were dismissed from Diss to form a church. The chapel dates from 1822 (the porch was added later). One story is that it was built as a thank-offering by an individual who had been saved from drowning in the River Waveney. As early as 1820 the church was providing preaching services at Pulham, and licensing a house at Harleston for weeknight meetings. The chapel seated 250, and in 1851 reported an afternoon congregation of 200.

Decline followed, and in 1919 the church ceased to meet and the chapel closed. Work was restarted by the Suffolk and Norfolk Association in 1924, and a small church re-formed in 1929 which joined the association for the first time. It failed to grow and work came to an end again in 1941. After closure, the chapel was sold in 1951. It was used at first by a breakaway group from the Church of England known as English Catholics, but by 1959 it passed to the Roman Catholics. It retained its two side galleries and most of the original box pews for many years. Today it is a private dwelling.

Location: Low Rd; OS grid ref.: TM275843

For further information

'A Chapel at Wortwell', *East Anglian Daily Times*, 24 December 1958

Records

NRO: FC93/1–4 (microfilm MF1618/8–9 etc), minutes, registers, members list etc., 1819–1901

Aldringham, Providence

A postcard of the 1812 chapel; these were sold before 1915 to raise money for the fund to build a replacement.

The Aldringham church was founded in 1812. Its first pastor, Robert Wilson, was the brother of the Tunstall pastor, Daniel Wilson, and had been evangelizing Aldeburgh and nearby villages. Rooms used for preaching were proving inadequate, but local opposition meant that the only possible site for a chapel was on the heath between several villages. Here the first Providence Chapel was erected. A schoolroom was added in 1814. A neighbouring landowner opposed the Baptists and planted trees on three sides of the chapel, which provided welcome seclusion. Like its parent, Aldringham soon gave birth to other churches, at Halesworth (1819), Aldeburgh (1819), Saxmundham (1823) and Friston (1829). By the 1840s there were regular prayer meetings in Eastbridge, Leiston and Knodishall, and by 1844 there were 114 members. No return was submitted for the 1851 religious census; perhaps its seclusion caused it to be overlooked by the enumerators!

A gallery had been added in 1818 and the chapel enlarged in 1855, but by 1903 it was becoming unsafe; those in the gallery were asked to remain seated for the hymns lest it collapse when they all stood up. A replacement was therefore designed by Cecil Lay ARIBA, built by G.A. Smyth of Leiston, and opened in 1915. The design paid considerable attention to external detail, and the large windows made for a light interior.

A group from Aldringham opened Union Chapel, **Aldeburgh**, in 1822, possibly replacing a Jireh Chapel registered in 1816. Union joined the SBU in the late 1840s, but another Baptist mission chapel (at 70 High St) was built in 1823 and rebuilt in 1878. Its fortunes fluctuated, and it closed by 1916, when it was taken over by the military. Sale followed in 1918. More recently it was used by W.M. Reade, the builders, but it does not appear to have survived.

In 1877 a schoolroom in Crown St, **Leiston**, was fitted up for mission services, the mission moving to Kings Rd in 1928. It was requisitioned during World War II and not released until 1949. An extension was built as late as 1972, but following the merger of the Aldringham and Leiston churches that year (see below) the premises came to be used primarily for youth work and were later sold.

A separate church was also started in Leiston in 1927, when the Aldringham pastor (John Hallum Barker) resigned, taking some of the congregation with him. Outreach in local villages, including the new resort of Thorpeness, could not prevent Aldringham experiencing a lengthy period of decline. Reconciliation with 'Faith', Leiston followed, under the ministry of Percy Marjoram. Since most of the congregation lived in Leiston, Aldringham was closed in 1976. Around 1980 the Association planned to convert it into a conference centre, and some work was done on the building, but the local authorities refused permission to modify it for that purpose. It is now a private dwelling, still with its graveyard.

Location: off Thorpeness Rd (B1353); OS grid ref.: TM457609

For further information

Anon., 'Aldringham Chapel sold', *G* July 1987, pp.8–9

G. T. Botwright, *Those Hundred and Fifty Years: A Ter-Jubilee History of the Strict Baptist Church at Aldringham, Suffolk*, n.pl., 1962

Israel Nichols, *The Origin of the Strict Baptist Chapel, Aldringham, Suffolk; with a few Particulars of its Past and Present: by a Sunday School Teacher*, London, 1895

Records

AGBC(EA): records etc, 1812–1973

SRO(I): FK2/6/1, register of marriages, 1915–46

TNA: RG4/1741, register of births, 1812–37

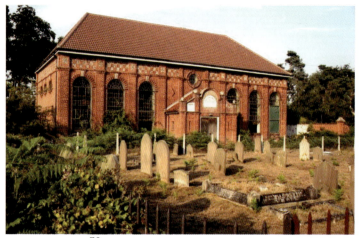

The chapel after closure and re-roofing (John Rushbrook)

Bardwell, Zion*

Work in Bardwell began when a house was certified in 1822 by the Bury St Edmunds church, and a local resident, Thomas Bullock, took a leading role. A church was formed here in 1824, and the chapel was erected that same year. A small building, with an equally small graveyard beside and to the rear, it nevertheless managed to seat 180; some would have used the gallery, though the size of the windows makes me think that there could not have been much headroom! The church was in membership with the Strict Baptist association from 1830 to 1853. In 1848 it reported 95 members, and two years later was maintaining three village preaching stations.

More recently, the church belonged to the Suffolk Baptist Union. Services ceased in 2003 (my father was the last pastor), and by 2011 the chapel was under conversion to residential use.

Location: Low St, IP31 1AS; OS grid ref.: TL940728

For further information

http://www.britishlistedbuildings.co.uk/en-284003-baptist-church-bardwell

Records

TNA: RG4/2823, births, 1820–37

Barrow, Cave Adullam

Standing in the middle of the village, this was built as a Congregational chapel, and registered in 1837. In the 1851 Religious Census it was designated simply as 'Trinitarian'. It is another of the few chapels in this book to be faced with flint, and located in a part of Suffolk which historically has not proved good soil for the Strict Baptists.

About 1995 it became the meeting place for a Strict Baptist congregation composed of seceders from the Gospel Standard cause at Lakenheath. The name which they gave it is not uncommon among Strict Baptist causes, and refers to the cave of Adullam, which was one of David's hiding places when fleeing from Saul (1 Samuel 22.1-2). To him came those in distress, in debt, or who were discontented.

Location: The Street; OS grid ref.: TL764635

Beccles, Martyrs' Memorial

The 1861 chapel (Keith Earles)

Particular Baptists were apparently present in Beccles from the 1730s, meeting in their own place of worship, but ceased to meet in the town in 1766; the remnant became part of the church at Claxton. The present church originated around 1803, when a group withdrew from the Independent chapel and were subsequently baptized by Job Hupton, the pastor at Claxton. Meeting in homes and then in a building known as the Cockpit (from its usage for cock-fighting), they erected a chapel behind some cottages in Newgate in 1805 and formed a church in 1808. Galleries were added to the chapel in 1814 and a lean-to extension at the front in 1834, and by 1851 it had a regular congregation of 400 morning and afternoon, and 320 in the evening, in a building which was claimed to seat 470. Gas lighting had been installed in 1845. The two decades from 1845 saw membership remain at over 200.

Following a number of brief pastorates and rejected calls to the pastorate, the church benefitted from a lengthy ministry. As well as being one of the chief architects of the Strict Baptist association, George Wright was the pastor from 1823 to 1870. Under his ministry the church grew and a replacement chapel became desirable, not least because of the state of the old one. A piece of land was donated by Sir Samuel Morton Peto, a local landowner (residing at Somerleyton Hall), railway contractor and benefactor of multitudes of Baptist causes, as well as treasurer of the Baptist Missionary Society. The new gault brick chapel was opened in 1861.

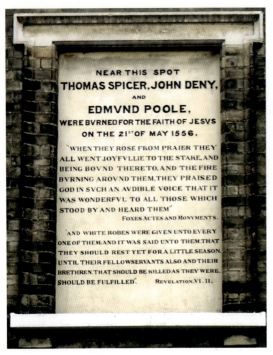

It is one of two Suffolk Strict Baptist chapels to bear a memorial tablet to sixteenth-century Protestant martyrs. Those commemorated here were burned in a meadow close by. The building and its monument were erected at a time when there was considerable unease nationally at the perceived spread of Catholic views, in the form of Roman Catholicism itself but also of high church or 'ritualistic' views and practices within the Church of England. Protestants reacted by erecting memorials to their forebears who had died during the reign of Queen Mary (1553-8). Moreover, in 1837 a local historian had remarked on the lack of a suitable memorial. Wright stated at the opening: 'It has been thought opportune at this time of Papal aggression in our favoured country to show our sympathy with these sufferers for Christ, by making the House of God commemorative of that event.'

In 1889 a schoolroom was added to the rear, and in 1938 the graveyard was levelled, with the headstones being placed around the edge of what became a car park. In recent years the name has been changed to Beccles Baptist Church, 'martyrs' having negative connotations in today's world.

Location: Station Rd, NR34 9QJ; OS grid ref.: TM424905

For further information

Anon., 'The "Martyrs' Memorial" – Baptist Chapel, Beccles', *GH* vol. 29 (1861), pp.100–2

Anon., *A Memorial to the Beccles Martyrs*, Beccles, 1956

Samuel K. Bland, *Memorials of George Wright, for forty-eight years Pastor of the Baptist Church at Beccles*, London, 1875

Derek Cooper, 'Profile of the Baptist Church at Beccles', *G* June 1988, pp.6–7

Keith Earles, *Beccles Baptist Church, 1808 to 2008: 200 Years of Christian Worship in Beccles*, Beccles, 2008

Noel M. Reeve, unpublished history, n.d.

www.becclesbaptistchurch.co.uk

Records

TNA: RG4/1833 births 1828–37

Bradfield St George

The old chapel (courtesy of Rachel Balmer, Bradfield and Rougham Baptist Church)

Bradfield owes its beginnings to the vision of Abi Last (1803–82), a young woman in service who returned to the village in 1834 and secured a promise from Cornelius Elven, pastor of the Particular Baptist church in Bury St Edmunds, that he would preach in the village if she could secure a room. In spite of opposition, much of it instigated by local Anglican clergy, a congregation was gathered together and a temporary chapel opened in 1835, behind a house in Freewood St; a church was formed in 1844. A permanent replacement was opened in 1850. Although not close to the village, the chapel occupied a prominent site on a road junction, accessible from several villages. Miss Last also built a schoolroom over the vestry (1868) and largely at her own expense maintained a day school taught by the pastor, which survived the 1870 Education Act by some years. The church joined the Strict Baptist association in 1866, where it has remained ever since.

In 1968 a new church hall was opened, but two years later the chapel required support by robust external buttresses added to the west wall. In 1980, therefore, a new chapel designed by Vivian Thrower, a member of Mount Zion, Ipswich, replaced the old one, on the same site but turned round by ninety degrees. During its building, the congregation was able to use the parish church on alternate Sunday mornings. Unusually, the chapel contains two stained glass windows, by Pippa Heskett of Shimpling, with the texts 'Ye must be born again' and 'Jesus said: follow me'.

Over time, the catchment area for the congregation has, like that for other chapels, widened, and the highest recorded membership figure (100) was not reached until the mid 1980s. The church continues to prosper, and so in 2012 it began a second Sunday morning service on the Moreton Hall estate in Bury St Edmunds, a large new suburban development.

Location: Kingshall Street, Rougham, IP30 9LG; OS grid ref.: TL917606

For further information

Anon., 'Church Profile: Bradfield and Rougham Baptist Church', *G* June 1986, pp.11–14

Anon., 'Memoir of Miss Abi. Last, late of Bradfield St. George, Suffolk', *GH* vol. 50 (1882), pp.328–31

John Doggett, 'Bradfield builds new …', *G* May 1980, pp.6–7

John Doggett, 'Young men shall see Visions', *G* June 1980, pp.13–14

SRO(B): John Duncan, 'The History of the Bradfield St George (Rougham) Baptist Chapel', typescript, 1965

Noel M. Reeve, unpublished history, 1996

Arthur Stone, *The Church in the Fields, 1834–1984: A History of Bradfield and Rougham Baptist Church, Bury St. Edmunds, Suffolk*, Bradfield, 1984

www.brbaptistchurch.info

Arthur Stone, who laid the foundation stone for the new chapel, did much to build up the work. He was typical of the Strict Baptist association in seeing no conflict between decidedly Calvinistic views and vigorous evangelistic activity.

Brockley

Like many rural chapels, Brockley sits in its own graveyard. Whilst this arrangement originated because Nonconformists were not allowed to be buried according to their own rites in the parish churchyards until 1880, it means that today they are oases of quietness, bearing their own testimony to the communion of saints. A number of my mother's family lie buried here, including my great-grandfather Marsh's five sons named after hymnwriters.

Houses in the village had been registered for worship by members at Bury in 1809 and 1833; in the latter year a chapel was registered for worship and in 1841 a church formed. The chapel was built on land donated by a local landowner, who also loaned the infant congregation the money to build. Although faced with brick, the building may be of clay lump construction, in which case it has survived remarkably well. Inside, a rear gallery was added in 1858. Electricity arrived in 1955, and an extension was added in 1967 with a kitchen and toilets. Sunday school facilities were provided in 1973.

The church remained outside the various associations until 1931, when it joined the Suffolk and Norfolk. Since then, the highest reported membership was 42, in 1955. Sadly, the congregation has declined considerably during the past two decades; population mobility can bring real problems for rural congregations.

Location: Chapel Lane, Brockley Green, IP29 4AS; OS grid ref.: TL824546

Work at **Rede** seems to have begun before World War I, and premises were purchased in 1927. It may have been intermittent, for he Sunday School was 'reopened' in 1950. However, Rede is a tiny village, and it was perhaps inevitable that the mission hall should finally close in 1985. It was sold soon after.

Location: OS grid ref.: TL805559

The chapel at **Hawstead** (on the Bury road) was built in 1923, and by 1929 was under the oversight of the Brockley church. Work ceased during the late 1960s, and the chapel was demolished after 1989.

Hawstead mission hall (courtesy of Mrs J. Grass)

For further information

Simon Ladd, 'Church Profile: Brockley Baptist Church, Suffolk – 150 Years Old', G June 1991, pp.15–18

Noel M. Reeve, unpublished history, 2002

Bungay, Bethesda

Twice the church at Beccles dismissed members to form a church in the town, in 1823 (nothing is known of what happened to this work), and again in 1846. On the latter occasion George Wright, pastor at Beccles, had been preaching in the town. For two years, John Hazelton was the pastor. Initially, the congregation met in the Corn Exchange, the chapel being opened in 1851. It was built (in under four months) to plans and specifications by Samuel Matthews of Lindsey, near Hadleigh. The church was in membership with the Suffolk and Norfolk Association from 1849 until 1901. By then the church had already begun to decline from its highest membership figure of 86, reported in 1891, and it was to have no pastor after 1899.

During World War I the church refused to insure the building against war damage, believing that God would protest it; it was as well that a change of mind took place, as the building was subsequently damaged. As for World War II, Noel Reeve records a striking incident:

> Thanks was given by the church later on when meeting for the Harvest thanksgiving Service on a Wednesday enemy bombers were busy over the town when bombs were dropped and the chapel windows were damaged, but gratefully no one was injured. The story was told to the writer by one who was there on that occasion of how several bombs were dropped in a row at regular intervals, had one more dropped in the same pattern the chapel would almost certainly have

received a direct hit, while this was happening, the congregation were singing the last verse of John Ryland's hymn, which goes,

> Plagues and deaths around me fly;
> Till He bids I cannot die;
> Not a single shaft can hit
> Till the God of love sees fit.

By the 1950s the church was very low, and began to receive help from Beccles. My father recalled taking Sunday services at Bungay during the early 1960s and being distracted during the morning by the smell of lunch wafting in from a room behind the chapel. Curiously, a garden to the side of the chapel was still being maintained at that time. Closure came in 1966, and since then the building has been used as a garage.

Location: Chaucer St (formerly Neatgate St), NR35 1DT; OS grid ref.: TM335898

A Gospel Standard cause was also in existence at Bungay by 1862, sharing a pastor with Zoar from 1887 to 1908. However, it appears to have closed fairly soon after that, as a result of the pastor's death.

For further information

Noel M. Reeve, unpublished history, 2002

Records

SBHS: church books, 1852–1960; membership list, c.1846–1939

Bury St Edmunds, Rehoboth

The Particular Baptist church in Bury was the parent of several Strict Baptist causes, and itself practised strict communion until 1855, but chose to join what later became the Suffolk Baptist Union. Perhaps inevitably, therefore, in 1837 a group holding Strict Baptist views broke away from Garland Street to found a new cause, meeting at first in the meat market and from 1838 (in which year a church was formed) in an auction room in Skinner St. The curiously shaped chapel was built in 1840 and named Rehoboth ('the Lord has made room for us'). The name is perhaps significant, since it was given to a well dug by Isaac's servants after local herdsmen had quarrelled with them over two previous wells they had dug (Genesis 26.22). In other words, the new chapel was believed by its founders to be God's provision, in which they could conduct their church life as they felt right.

However, the church never prospered; its highest membership was 53, reported as early as 1842. It joined the Strict Baptist association on its foundation but left in 1851. It was omitted from that year's Religious Census, although it was certainly active for some years after that. A re-formation took place in 1877, and the church briefly rejoined the association around 1896, finally coming into membership once more in 1931, by which time it had become very weak. It is perhaps remarkable that the cause lasted as long as it did, not closing until 1951. The chapel was soon sold and converted into offices, but its original use is still proclaimed by the stone over the front entrance.

Location: 16 Out Westgate, IP33 3NZ; OS grid ref.: TL852637

For further information

J. Duncan, typescript history of Garland St (1963), includes summary of Rehoboth

J. Duncan, 'The Origins of the Free Churches in Bury St Edmunds', 2 vols, typescript, 1955, pt. 12

Records

SBHS: minutes, 1895–6

Charsfield

A cottage was licensed for worship in 1804 by the Otley pastor, and the church was formed in 1809 with the dismissal of members from Grundisburgh. The chapel was built in 1808. Growth followed, and the front wall was brought forward in 1846; from the side it is possible to see where this was done. Over the entrances is inscribed, in two parts, Psalm 100.4: 'Enter into his gates with thanksgiving, and into his courts with praise'. Inside, the baptistery is set at right angles to the pulpit; one wonders whether the communion table would have been placed above it. The church joined the Strict Baptist association in 1849 with a membership of 110, and in 1851 average attendances were stated to be 236 in the mornings, 318 in the afternoons, and just 50 in the evenings. But by 1923 things had declined to the extent that a Home Missionary was placed there; happily it revived. In 1930 it was reported that a plot had been secured for a Sunday School building; on the opposite side of the road to the chapel a new hall was erected in 1972, which had formerly been a prefabricated bungalow. In 2000 it was replaced with a new building.

Location: The Street, IP13 7PY; OS grid ref.: TM258563

For further information

Tim Barker, *The Baptist Church at Charsfield 1808-2008*, Charsfield, 2008

Peter Matthias, 'The 1930s remembered: A Suffolk Country Church', *G* January 1990, pp.19–20

Noel M. Reeve, unpublished history, 1997

Records

SRO(I): FK2/5/1, marriages, 1983–5

Chelmondiston

The church here was formed by dismissal of members from Stoke Green, Ipswich, in 1825; that church had itself moved from nearby Woolverstone in 1775, so Baptists were early active in the area. The first place of worship was converted from what had been a store for coal and grain, which had a wooden upper storey; it was known as the 'Chelmondiston Coal Hole'. The unpromising nickname did not hinder the work, and various alterations proved necessary. In 1827 the open side was bricked up and the granary floor taken away, to allow seating at ground floor level. Further modifications were made in 1839, and in 1854 a complete rebuilding took place. In 1858 a day school was being provided here. The chapel was severely damaged by a flying bomb in December 1944, but rebuilt.

Congregations in 1851 were 3-400 morning and afternoon, but just 60 in the evening. The church was in membership with the Suffolk and Norfolk association from 1845 to 1858 (when it reported a membership of 173), and has latterly been linked with the Suffolk and Norfolk's Sunday School Branch. Services ceased in 2006, but the chapel has since reopened as part of an endeavour to plant a congregation under the auspices of the Grace Baptist Partnership, a modern equivalent of nineteenth-century home missionary societies; a church was formed in 2011.

Location: Pin Mill Rd, IP9 1JE; OS grid ref.: TM206373

For further information

Anon., *A Brief History of the Strict and Particular Baptist Church Chelmondiston*, c.1963

www.gracebaptistpartnership.org.uk/planting-churches-2/chelmondiston/

Records

TNA: RG4/1835 & 3924, births, 1810–34, 1831–7; burials, 1831–4

Clare*

This, like several other early causes in Suffolk, had its roots in the local Independent church. In 1801 it was decided to dissolve this and form a Baptist congregation, but this was not done, and so in 1803 the Baptists seceded and formed a new church. A chapel was opened in 1805, and a replacement in 1821. The present chapel, with its classical façade, bears the date 1859, although it may incorporate remnants of its predecessor. It retained its original box pews downstairs until as late as 1988.

Congregations in 1851 were in the order of 450 morning and afternoon and 60 in the evening, the small attendance at night being fairly typical of Suffolk chapels. As usual, the church was active in outreach to neighbouring communities. In 1851 it purchased a chapel at Hundon jointly with the Independents, and did the same thing at Stoke by Clare in 1853. In 1859 it agreed to collaborate with both Glemsford Strict Baptist churches to hold meetings at Cavendish.

Throughout the nineteenth century it seems to have remained Strict Baptist in its practice (it was in the Suffolk and Norfolk association from 1859 until 1868, when membership was around 120), but it then joined the Suffolk Baptist Union.

Location: High St, CO10 8NY; OS grid ref.: TL769455

The old burial ground survives, some way from the chapel on the road to Cavendish

For further information

Lionel F. Higgs, *One Hundred Years of Witness: The Story of Clare Baptist Church*, Clare, 1960

David Ridley, *Clare Baptist Church: The First 200 Years*, Clare, 2003

www.clarebaptistchurch.org.uk

Records

TNA: RG4/2127, deaths, 1822–35

Cransford

The old chapel (courtesy of Philip Kettle, Cransford Christian Fellowship)

Cransford is one of several churches which came into existence as a result of the activity of a local builder, George Denny Spratt, who had been sent out to preach by the church at Wortwell; others were at Friston and Fressingfield, and he was also responsible for restarting work at Laxfield. While living at Hacheston, Spratt began preaching in a cottage; when it ceased to be available, a barn at Cransford was fitted out for services. In 1838 a nucleus of members were dismissed from Tunstall and elsewhere to form a church here, and a chapel was opened in 1841. It is one of the few churches to have belonged to the Suffolk and Norfolk Association since being formed. Work was assisted initially by the Suffolk Baptist Home Missionary Society. A division seems to have occurred around 1863, but not to have lasted.

On 18 October 1987, the chapel was destroyed by a hurricane. The church met in the village hall until a replacement, seating 90, was completed in 1990.

Cransford has never been a large church, its highest membership being 66 in 1858, but it remains vigorous. As well as providing the only opportunity for weekly worship in the village, the building offers a valuable community facility, an example of the uses to which village chapels can be put.

Location: Cransford, IP13 9NZ; OS grid ref.: TM318647

Cransford maintained several village stations until the 1970s. One (opened in 1958 after intermittent work in the village since 1948) used the waiting room of the old railway station at **Parham** for a Sunday School, but work in Parham and Hacheston ceased after 1976. A Primitive Methodist chapel was built at **Badingham** in 1836. According to the 1851 Religious Census, it seated 110 with standing room for 30 others, though its isolated position makes one wonder where they came from! The Cransford church was working in the village around 1904, and evangelistic services were held in 1926, but in 1948 this chapel was purchased by the churches at Cransford and Laxfield. Work ceased in 1988, and the chapel is now a private dwelling, retaining its noticeboard.

Location: High Rd (A1120), east of the village; OS grid ref.: TM 327682

John Rushbrook

For further information

Anon., 'Cransford Chapel Demolished', *G* December 1987, p.12

Bob Allison, 'Rebuilding at Cransford', *G* June 1989, p.11

Noel M. Reeve, unpublished history, 1996

G January 1990

Crowfield, Bethesda

The chapel as it appeared during the mid twentieth century (Ralph Chambers, courtesy of the SBHS)

A house was certified for worship here in 1823, and a meeting house registered the following year. The present chapel was built in 1834 and enlarged in 1835; it is still possible to see from the brickwork where this was done. The church was formed when nineteen members were dismissed from Stoke Green, Ipswich, in 1836.

A reference in the report of a ministerial induction here in 1857 to a service being held at the old 'Cave Adullam' at Winston (where there were many Dissenters) implies that the congregation, or a part of it, may have met previously in that village.

The church belonged to the Suffolk and Norfolk Association from 1844 to 1855, withdrawing because it alleged that some churches were not adhering to the association's articles of faith. Like a number of others it preferred to exist independently, only rejoining in 1949.

A vestry was added to the rear of the chapel in 1877, and on a plot of land further back there is a modern hall (1980).

Location: Stone St, IP6 9SZ; OS grid ref.: TM149570

This picture shows how the building has been enlarged at various points.

In 1952 a building fund was started to provide a mission hall at the hamlet of **Gosbeck**, and a wooden construction was opened the next year. Work here ceased in 1989 and the hall was sold in 1996. It still stands, in a private garden.

Location: OS grid ref.: TM163560

For further information

Noel M. Reeve, unpublished history, 1997

http://crowfieldbc.onesuffolk.net

Earl Soham

An unidentified place of worship was registered here in 1800, but there is no evidence as to whether this was a forerunner of later Baptist work in the village carried out by the church at Horham. The first chapel here was built in 1821 by one Robert Mullenger, and became known as the Black Chapel. It is a weatherboarded construction (relatively unusual for a chapel in this area), with a pyramidal slate roof. The church was formed the same year. In 1828 it was reported that unless the church could raise sufficient funds to purchase the chapel, which was private property, they would lose the use of it, and sister churches were urged to take up collections in support. Once sufficient funds had been raised, a trust was established to prevent a repetition.

By 1851, the chapel, which had a reported seating capacity of 200, was attracting average congregations of 100 in the morning and 150 in the afternoon. It ceased to be used in 1859 when the church moved to a brick-built chapel (pictured overleaf), and was sold, complete with internal fittings, in 1878. At one point it was being used as a store. Remarkably, it still stands, down an alley off the main A1120, and is Grade II listed. By 2012 it was under conversion as a dwelling.

The church was part of the Strict Baptist association from 1840 until 1863, when it had a membership of 76. More recently it has belonged to the Baptist Union and its local association. The second chapel ceased to be used for worship in 2009 and the congregation moved to Framlingham. Like the first, by 2012 it was being converted for residential use.

Work at **Brandeston** began around 1840. This became one of five village stations operated by the Earl Soham church. In 1850 the church was offered the use on Sunday evenings of the Independent

Chapel, built in 1838. Oddly enough, its reported congregation in 1851 was larger than that of the parent church. This chapel too is now a house.

Locations: 'Black Chapel', Little Green; OS grid ref.: TM231630

(second chapel) Low Rd (just off A1120); OS grid ref.: TM229631

(Brandeston) The Street; OS grid ref.: TM245608

For further information

www.pastscape.org.uk/hob.aspx?hob_id=1495710#aSt, accessed 3 July 2012

Records

SRO(I): FK2/500/3/9, misc.

SRO(I): HB84/2/4/1/1/17/10, deeds etc, 1826 onwards

Fressingfield*

The first chapel in the village was opened in 1819, probably in a barn at Church Farm. The work seems to have had links with churches at Horham and Stradbroke. In 1833, George Denny Spratt, whom we encountered at Cransford, moved to Wortwell from Friston, and got involved with the developing work at Fressingfield.

Fressingfield is one of two Strict Baptist chapels in Suffolk to be built to a hexagonal, almost coffin-shaped, design; the other was Friston. However, the story that the design was intended to remind worshippers of their mortality appears incorrect. Spratt (who became the first pastor, preaching without charge for twenty years) wanted a building which would accommodate the maximum number of people and enable them to hear the preaching, but with the minimum of expense (he was, after all, building it himself). The result was an edifice which, he stated in 1851, could seat about 650 and which regularly saw an afternoon congregation of 400–600. An extension at the rear (rebuilt around 1985) is noteworthy for using a similar shape.

A church was formed in 1839, apparently by dismissal of members from Wortwell; Spratt then sold the chapel to the new church. The chapel was reseated downstairs in 1910, when the pulpit was replaced and the brick floor replaced by a board floor with block flooring in the aisles. The pulpit is located on the wall opposite the front entrance, and a gallery runs right round the chapel. The pews downstairs were replaced by chairs in 1985.

From 1857 the church was in membership with the Strict Baptist association, although it was occasionally suggested that it should withdraw. Quite possibly its Calvinism was, like that of other churches along the Norfolk/Suffolk border, of an even higher stamp than that of the associated churches. In 1925 the pastor resigned from the association, and shortly afterwards from the church. He may have influenced it to withdraw, which it did in 1927 on the grounds that it considered the association was failing to contend for the truth. However, it is clear that opinion on this step was never unanimous. For a few years from 1935 it appeared on the Gospel Standard list of causes, having disavowed its former links with 'the Earthen Vessel denomination'.

By the 1960s membership had sunk from a peak of 86 in 1912 and 1924 to about a dozen, and did not begin to recover until the late 1970s, after which it rose to over 70. In recent years it has remained independent of any association, but maintains close links with local Strict Baptist congregations.

Location: Low Rd, IP21 5PE; OS grid ref.: TM263774

For further information

'Church Profile: Fressingfield', *G* March 1988, pp.8–11

David J. Steere, *The History of Fressingfield Baptist Chapel, 1835-1985*, [Fressingfield, 1985]

B.W. Clover, *Faithfulness and Fruit at Fressingfield: A Short History of the Strict Baptist Church, Fressingfield*, Harleston, 1935

http://fressbc.wordpress.com

Friston

In 1829, sixteen members were dismissed from Aldringham to begin a work here. They met in a cottage, being formed into a church in 1830. Growth necessitated their removal to a barn the same year. A chapel was needed, and George Denny Spratt on moving to the village was conscious of this. In 1831 the foundation stone was laid by Cornelius Elven of a chapel built to Spratt's distinctive hexagonal design (hence its current name, Hexagon Baptist Chapel); the building was registered in 1834. In 1851 it was said to seat 450 and to have an average afternoon attendance of almost that. Membership rose to 103 by 1855 before beginning a long decline to a low point of 6 in 1950; doubtless agricultural depression and rural depopulation played their parts in this. The pastor from 1834 to 1888 was William Brown, who had studied and practised architecture, although he does not appear to have designed any Suffolk chapels.

During the 1970s the seating downstairs had to be renewed, and all pews now face the pulpit instead of some being sideways on. Until then there had been an unusual trapezoidal communion table and pew.

The church was in membership of the old association for just a year (1830). It then joined the new, with which it remained until 2009.

Location: Mill Rd, IP17 1PH; OS grid ref.: TM410601

For further information

F.C. Ward, *The History of the Friston Baptists 1831-1981*, Friston, 1981

www.fristonbaptistsuffolk.org.uk

Records

SBHS: minutes 1879-1906

The front of the chapel (courtesy of Marcus Keogh-Brown, Friston Baptist Church)

Glemsford, Ebenezer*

The church at Bury St Edmunds was active in the upper Stour valley from the early years of the nineteenth century, and by 1828 a work had been established at Glemsford. Ebenezer Chapel was built in 1829, and a church formed in 1830 by 44 members from Bury. It joined the Strict Baptist association in 1842 but withdrew ten years later. By 1846 membership had climbed to 153, and in 1851 average afternoon attendance was said to be 420, slightly above the chapel's seating capacity.

Division came in 1859; the pastor until 1858, Robert Barnes, had been much loved and inevitably in the eyes of many he was what we should call 'a hard act to follow'. His proposed successor, Jonathan Mose, did not receive the approval of all and so was advised by the association (which the church rejoined in 1859) to leave. The seceders met in a barn before building Providence Chapel, a few hundred yards up the road. Ebenezer withdrew from the association again in 1871, not returning until 1923, by which time membership had fallen below 20.

Deterioration of the chapel necessitated its closure in 1988 with a view to demolition and replacement. Preservation societies objected, and it was listed and sold, becoming a private residence. The church met in the Brethren hall along the street until 1992, when it ceased to exist; although its last few years had seen growth, it had been forced to shelve the search for a new site.

Location: Egremont St; OS grid ref.: TL828475

For further information

J. Duncan, 'Suffolk Free Church History', vol. II, typescript, n.d.

Records

AGBC(EA): Minutes, 1826–1936, etc

Glemsford, Providence

Providence Chapel on Hunt's Hill was built in 1859 and a church formed by 25 seceders from Ebenezer. The building was of red brick, with yellow brick dressings and lancet windows. The SBU agreed in 1861 to invite the church to join it, but it never joined any association and remained Strict Baptist in its outlook, possibly more high Calvinist in ethos than was Ebenezer. In 1910 Ebenezer raised the possibility of a merger of the two churches, but Providence did not wish to do so. The chapel closed in 1965 and by 1977 it had been demolished, but the burial ground is still maintained.

Location: Hunt's Hill; OS grid ref.: TL829479

For further information

www.foxearth.org.uk/glemsfordPictures/oldchurch.jpg

SRO(B): K552, photograph, 1906

Records

SBHS: minutes, 1859–1911

Great Ashfield, Bethel

Very little is known about the chapel at Great Ashfield, although the church was in membership of the Strict Baptist association from 1849 to 1873. It is not even certain when it was formed, various dates between 1838 and 1848 being offered. However, we do know that a house was certified for worship by Cornelius Elven of Bury in 1841, and that the Wetherden church began work in the village about 1843. According to the 1851 Religious Census, the chapel was erected in 1848 and had seating for 120, with average congregations of 60 (and 28 scholars) in the mornings and 100 in the afternoons.

In 1855 the church hosted the annual tent meetings, and its report to the association took the opportunity to present its needs, as being 'in a very low and unpromising condition, and so we apprehend it will remain till some better place of worship, in a more convenient locality, be erected'. In 1862, the church petitioned the association for help in purchasing the chapel and a piece of ground on which to extend it, but the circular letter expressed the opinion that members would be better advised to join with other local churches, since the chapel was inconveniently located and the church unable to support a pastor. The church was still active as late as 1889, but the chapel, which was situated well away from the village, has since been demolished.

Great Blakenham

A Baptist chapel was registered in the village in 1839. At the time of the 1851 Religious Census its minister was John Corley of Ipswich; it reported congregations of 73 in the morning and 101 in the afternoon. However, the work died out, and the present church represents a fresh start.

Two cottages were converted for meetings but they became too small, and in 1873 a new chapel was purpose-built, largely thanks to William Houghton, who became the first pastor. Their previous meeting-place became a school and then a blacksmith's shop. A baptistery was put in and stabling added in 1882, a new vestry was added in 1928, and a school hall in 1949. The church was formed in 1876 and has belonged to the Suffolk and Norfolk Association since 1889. Its location near a large town may help to explain why its highest membership (75) was not reached until 1917; possibly the village suffered less from depopulation since there alternative sources of employment were at hand.

Location: Chapel Lane, IP6 0JJ; OS grid ref.: TM126501

For further information

R.G. Prime, *Gt. Blakenham Baptist Chapel 1873–1973*, Great Blakenham, 1973

Noel M. Reeve, unpublished history, 1996

G June 1973, p.17

Records

SRO(B): FK2/11, marriages, 1983–90

Grundisburgh

Baptist activity here began when a builder named Stephen Lawrence invited Mr George from Beaumont Chapel in Woodbridge (part of the Countess of Huntingdon's Connexion), to preach, and built a chapel adjoining his house in 1796. George's ministry had not met with approval in Woodbridge and seems to have been no more successful in Grundisburgh. Initial interest waned until late in 1797, when John Thompson, a local farmer who belonged to Stoke Green, Ipswich, began preaching here. The chapel soon became too small, and in 1798 a new one was built at Thompson's expense, on the same site as the old one and reusing some materials from it. A church was formed with 43 members dismissed from Stoke Green.

Within ten years its membership had increased to 386. During the early nineteenth century, it was responsible for planting congregations over a wide catchment area. This period was one of great activity among the more evangelical Dissenters, as they took full advantage of increased freedoms to spread the gospel and found new congregations. However, opposition was sometimes intense, as when riots occurred at Wickham Market in 1810; these events, and the dilatory nature of the resulting court proceedings, helped to bring about the formation of the Protestant Society for the Protection of Religious Liberty.

At one point during Thompson's ministry, members were drawn from no less than 55 parishes, and the congregation numbered 800. By 1825, it was claimed that a third of households in Grundisburgh were Baptist. The chapel had to be enlarged twice: in 1810 a schoolroom and vestry was built at the side, and a few years later a small extension to that was added. A pair of cottages was purchased by the stream at Playford, and baptisms were conducted here for some years until 1816.

A number of daughter churches were formed (though not all would become Strict Baptist): Otley (1800), Framsden (1800), Tunstall (1805), Charsfield (1809), Sutton (1810), Woodbridge (1820), Providence, Ipswich (1824), and East Bergholt (1826). In those days, a newly formed church did not wait long before replicating the process which had led to its own formation.

When, about 1816, serious economic troubles beset Thompson, he had to sell the chapel, but it was repurchased and later put in trust. He died in 1826, but was followed by Samuel Collins, whose pastorate lasted from 1827 to 1876. Under his ministry membership reached a peak of 359 in 1848. A day school was also established in 1847, which catered for 70 children.

Thompson baptized almost 660 people during his ministry and Collins around 400. However, baptisms took place at Culpho Hall, where Thompson had lived, as the chapel appears not to have had a baptistery at this time.

Collins's major contribution, however, was as an officer of the Strict Baptist association, which was founded here in 1829 (although the church did not join until slightly later). This perhaps explains the quotation from the apostle Paul on his memorial tablet: 'in labours abundant ... beside the care of all the churches' (2 Corinthians 11.23, 28).

> TO THE
> HONOURED AND BELOVED
> MEMORY OF
> SAMUEL COLLINS,
> NEARLY FIFTY YEARS PASTOR
> OF THIS CHURCH
> BORN AT CULWORTH, NORTHAMPTONSHIRE,
> DECEMBER 22ND 1798,
> FIRST PREACHED IN GRUNDISBURGH
> NOVEMBER 27TH 1826,
> CHOSEN TO THE PASTORATE
> NOVEMBER 18TH 1827,
> RESIGNED 1876,
> FELL ASLEEP (AT EYE) JULY 17TH 1881.
> "IN LABOURS MORE ABUNDANT..
> BESIDE THE CARE OF ALL THE CHURCHES."

The chapel is one of the best surviving examples of any in this book of a 'meeting house' plan, in which the pulpit is placed on a long wall with the main entrance facing it. Doors in the side walls give access to large galleries round three sides of the chapel. The building was refronted in 1863, and additional accommodation was provided for the Sunday School in 1897, though it is unclear whether this replaced or added to the earlier extensions noted above.

Around 1900 the church gave help to the weak cause at Beaumont and a Baptist Union church was formed; it seems likely that Grundisburgh was rather open in its outlook at this time, and it withdrew from the Suffolk and Norfolk Association in 1907, rejoining in 1921. However, by now it was, like so many village causes, in decline, and membership had fallen to the thirties by 1945. Yet as late as 1904 there were eight village stations, and my father recalled conducting cottage meetings at Swilland around 1965. By the 1960s, the church was receiving help from the Home Mission. In recent years it has seen a slight measure of growth, thanks to a settled pastoral ministry, and in 1990 the interior was modified, the galleries being partitioned off and the pews replaced by chairs.

Location: Chapel Lane, IP13 6TS; OS grid ref.: TM227502

For further information

SBHS: 'The history of Grundisburgh Baptist Chapel', [slide script, c.1960]

Peter Bishop, *Grundisburgh: The History of a Suffolk Village*, Swavesey, 1992, pp.45–50

S.K. Bland, 'Early Days of the Grundisburgh Church', *GH* vol. 50 (1882), pp.207–10

Samuel K. Bland, *An Outline of the History for One Hundred Years of the Baptised Church of Christ at Grundisburgh*, Woodbridge, 1898

[A.K. Cowell], *A Short Biographical Account of the late Mr. John Thomson [sic], Many Years Pastor of the Baptist Church, Grundisburgh, Suffolk, comprising an Account of the Riots and Persecution attending the Introduction of the Gospel into Wickham-Market, In the Year 1810*, Ipswich, 1827

Colin Grimwood, *200 Years of God's Work at Grundisburgh Baptist Church*, Grundisburgh, 1998

Nigel Lacey & Colin Grimwood, 'Solid Building at Grundisburgh', *G* October 1993, pp.6-7

Hilda Tuck, *Pernicious Dissenters: The Story of John Thompson of Culpho, 1755–1826*, n.d.

Sydney Wolstenholme, 'Grundisburgh – Mother of Many', *G* March 1989, p.13

www.woodbridgechurch.org.uk/Records/beaumont.htm

www.grundisburghchapel.org.uk

Records

SRO(I): J419/5, microfilms of birth certificates, 1828-37

For the Suffolk and Norfolk Association's centenary meetings here in 1930, this commemorative postcard was issued

Hadleigh*

The church was formed by dismissal of a number of members from Wattisham in 1815, but its fortunes fluctuated. In 1830 the present chapel (the second) was opened, but was closed for some months in 1842–3, before being reopened by the Suffolk Baptist Home Missionary Society. In 1848 the church was reported to have been dissolved, a number of members joining that at Wattisham, but was re-formed in 1851, growing to 104 members by 1888. A schoolroom was added to the chapel in 1876 and a gallery in 1884, and the chapel was refloored and reseated in 1897/8. Yet by 1905 the cause had again become a mission station, and the chapel closed for a short period before the church was re-formed in 1916. Work continued under the oversight of an 'emergency committee' until the church was able to rejoin the association in 1926. An extension dating from the mid 1980s reflects the unusual arched bays of the chapel's frontage.

In 2008 the church (by now with almost 90 members) resigned its membership of the Suffolk and Norfolk Association; it is now linked with the Fellowship of Independent Evangelical Churches.

Location: George St, IP7 5BD; OS grid ref.: TM028426

For further information

'Church Profile: Hadleigh', *G* February 1984, pp.7–8

D. French, *History of Hadleigh Baptist Church, 1815–1980: Commemorating the 150th Anniversary of the erection of the Chapel in George Street, Hadleigh, Suffolk in 1830*, [Hadleigh, 1980]

www.hadleighbaptist.org.uk

Records

TNA: RG4/1841, births, 1821–37

Hadleigh Heath

Meetings in the locality began in a cottage in 1819, moving to a barn in 1823, the year that a church was formed, presumably from that at Hadleigh. In time the barn became too small and the landlord was also refusing to repair it, and so the chapel and the house adjoining were built in 1849,. The 1851 census return (which reported an afternoon attendance of no less than 185) describes it as having been built in 1801 at Hadleigh Heath and 'removed' to Polstead (in which parish Hadleigh Heath is situated) in 1849, but this may refer to the congregation rather than the building. Enlargement followed in 1871, but by 1888 it appears to have been in Brethren use (a Brethren assembly appears to have existed in Hadleigh by 1877 and to have been active in 1892). It was taken back under the wing of the Hadleigh church from 1892 to 1899 as a 'branch church'; there was a Sunday School here, and services on Sundays and weeknights. However, when the Hadleigh pastor, Abner Morling, moved away, the link appears to have ceased.

Little more is heard of the cause until the early 1960s, when the house was modernized, the work was revived (although it appears never to have closed), and a leader appointed. It had been run by non-members and only joined the Suffolk and Norfolk Association when they died. Sadly, the chapel's situation on a busy road away from habitation probably rendered closure inevitable, and by 1966 services were no longer being held. The chapel and house were sold in 1969, but the graveyard has continued to be maintained by the Hadleigh church and the association, an example of how such responsibilities often continue many years after closure and even demolition of a building.

Location: on A1071, 2 miles west of Hadleigh; OS grid ref.: TL998416

For further information

AGBC (EA): 'Hadleigh Heath Baptist Chapel, 1849–1949', typescript, 1949

Halesworth

The first meetings here took place in a house about 1816. The first chapel was registered for worship in 1820 for a church formed the previous year by dismissal of members from Aldringham. This building was actually located in the parish of Holton, and is now known as Kentread House. The church was a founder member of the new association, remaining in it until 1907.

Around 1836, a replacement was converted off Chediston St, which has not been traced. The first chapel was still listed in the 1861 census, presumably retained as a mission station. Its replacement was not well situated, for in 1854, soon after legislation was passed permitting religious services to be held in theatres and other such venues, the church reported that the local theatre had been hired by some of its members.

> We have always felt the approach to our chapel a great inconvenience on a dark night, and almost to preclude the possibility of expecting any who are not our regular attendants. The Theatre is much more convenient for the town-folks, and many there are who neglect altogether attending public worship. We earnestly hope to see some who would not, through prejudice or otherwise, enter a chapel, and who do not attend church.[1]

Growth seems to have come to the congregation, for the membership rose to 125 by 1866. Decline followed, partly due to recurrent internal dissension. In 1904 part of the Chediston St chapel was blown in during a winter storm, and services ultimately ceased about 1914.

Location: (first chapel) Loampit Lane; OS grid ref.: TM393778

Records

SRO(L): Acc.353/1, Halesworth Baptist Church, Minutes vol. 2, 1856–1903

---

[1] *GH* vol. 22 (1854), p.241.

Haverhill*

Work in this town began from the church at Sible Hedingham, a church being formed in 1828. The chapel was built the same year. In its early years it seems to have gone its own way; congregations in 1851 were no more than 20, and in 1853 the last remaining trustee was found to be living in the vestry. The building was purchased thereafter and properly vested in a trust. A two-storey extension comprising a gallery and vestry was added about 1860, giving the building a distinctive appearance, but the chapel was closed from 1862 to 1870 and possibly at a later point as well. The church appears to have been re-formed in 1870, and again in 1930. It has never belonged to either county association, but over recent decades has developed closer links with the Grace Baptists.

Location: Upper Downs Slade, CB9 8HF; OS grid ref.: TL670455

Records

SRO(B): IN500/64, Accounts for H. Richardson's charity, 1902–31

Horham

Standing in fields away from the village, you might be surprised on a Sunday to observe that this chapel has a thriving congregation and a membership of over a hundred. Work began when a local Independent member opened his house in Athelington for preaching. He was later baptized by Charles Farmery, pastor at Diss. The first chapel here was opened in 1799 (the church was formed the same year) and provided with galleries in 1807. The church was It may have been closed for a period before 1825, but by 1851 average attendance in the afternoon was as high as 600.

The present chapel dates from 1859. A gallery runs right round the building, the section behind the pulpit being shuttered. An extension was added in 1982 and a new hall across the lane in 1991. The church has always been Strict Baptist, but only joined the Suffolk and Norfolk Association in 1922.

Location: Chapel Lane, IP21 5ER; OS grid ref.: TM219715

Records

SRO(I): FK2/6/2-6, marriages 1910–63

SRO(I): IN400/101/2, John Knight's charity, returns, 1922–45

Hoxne

Work here began with occasional preaching from about 1814, a house being registered for worship in 1823. The chapel was opened in 1834; it seated 200 but congregations took a while to grow, the best attended service in 1851 attracting about 70 people. In 1845 it was reported that the church's application to join the new association had not been accepted, but it was received in 1859. By 1862, the minister and messengers reported to the association that the cause was so feeble that it would be best to close it, but a remarkable turnaround followed. A new chapel was opened in 1865 (possibly a thorough rebuild), but a vestry had to be added in 1866 and a gallery in 1869. Membership rocketed from 15 in 1865 to 84 in 1869. A new vestry with schoolroom above was added in 1883.

Around 1930 the church briefly withdrew from the Strict Baptists and joined the SBU, under the influence of its minister, W.H. Hercock. His application to join the association had been withdrawn in 1923; a deferred application in 1926 was rejected. It was normal for pastors to become personal members, and not to do so betokened disagreement with its principles and practice. Once he moved on, the church reverted to its original allegiance. The chapel closed in 2002, following the death some months earlier in a car accident of the minister in charge and his wife; it has since been converted to a private dwelling.

Location: Cross St; OS grid ref.: TM184761

For further information

Noel M. Reeve, unpublished history, 2002

Records

AGBC(EA): Minute books, accounts, etc, 1869–1982

SRO(I): HD405/1, Charles Masterson (pastor), diary, 1865–72

Ipswich, Bethesda*

In 1829, twenty members were dismissed from the Baptist church at Stoke Green to form a new congregation. They met briefly in a former Wesleyan chapel in Long Lane before purchasing a chapel in Dairy Lane. This had been converted from cottages in 1792 for use by a group of Independents associated with the Countess of Huntingdon's Connexion, who had seceded from the church in Tacket St. Interestingly, the first Independent minister at Dairy Lane was Job Hupton, who adopted Baptist views and pastored the Baptist church at Claxton in 1794 until his death in 1849.

Three years later, the chapel was extended, but division in 1841 saw it closed for a few months, and another Strict Baptist church formed, which became Zoar. The association circular letter for 1842 reports this as a move of the existing church: what seems to have happened is that the majority went with the new cause, while the rump also left the Dairy Lane chapel and met in Rope Walk.

The picture above shows the position of the old chapel (courtesy of Bethesda Baptist Church, Ipswich); the picture below is taken from the booklet produced in 1913 to mark the new chapel's opening

In 1851 it was reported that the chapel was seeing congregations of 450 in the morning, 650 in the afternoon, and 400 in the evening. One suspects that it was not a comfortable place in which to worship and since a later estimate gave the seating capacity as just 300, it was probably overcrowded. By 1900 it was becoming unsafe, and rebuilding was deemed imperative. A school hall was built first, as the church adopted a gradual approach to the building project. The chapel itself went ahead after a donor, a Bristol solicitor named A.W. Page, undertook to bear the entire cost in memory of his mother. C.H. Spurgeon, whose preference was for classical over Gothic designs, would heartily have approved this new building, the columns of which are reminiscent of Spurgeon's own Metropolitan Tabernacle in London. It was designed by Frederick G. Faunch, LRIBA (a member of the Strict Baptist church at Gurney Road, Stratford), and opened in 1913. Seating a thousand people, the internal woodwork was of English oak and a fine organ was provided. Apparently, the architect's original plan had the chapel facing Fonnereau Road with a schoolroom underneath and a manse towards the road junction, but the plan was altered after it was decided to build the schoolroom first. The confidence expressed by the building was justified, and the church grew to a membership of 807 in 1968, although it is rather smaller now.

Several twentieth-century ministers had problems with the practice of strict communion, and eventually the church moved away from it. Since 2000 it is no longer in membership with the Grace Baptist association, but remains active on its commanding site. In 1999, it acquired a seventeenth-century public house, the Running Buck, and converted it into a coffee shop and meeting venue.

Location: Fonnereau Rd, IP4 2BB; OS grid ref.: TM165449

For further information

Charles R. Clarke, *A New Heart for the Old [Running] Buck*, Ipswich, 2000

A.E. Garrard et al., *Bethesda Chapel, Ipswich*, Ipswich, 1913

A.E. Garrard, *A Short History of 'Bethesda', Ipswich*, Ipswich, 1924

Frederick G. Smith, *The Bethesda Story*, Ipswich, 1963

Frederick G. Smith, *The Bethesda Story Retold*, Ipswich, 1988

Gladys Southgate, 'Sunday School Anniversaries at Bethesda Chapel, Ipswich', *G* Apr 1978, pp.9–10

www.bethesdaipswich.co.uk

www.thekeyipswich.co.uk

Records

TNA: RG4/1850, births, 1813–37 (includes Independents)

Ipswich, Mount Zion / Cauldwell Hall Road

In 1894 a group of Strict Baptists began to use a 'Zionist' mission hall in Cauldwell Hall Road. It was known as Cave Adullam, taken to apply to 'a fold of wandering sheep'. The work prospered, and a church was formed in 1909. Three years later the mission hall was replaced by Mount Zion chapel (in the picture). The church joined the Suffolk and Norfolk Association in 1923, having first applied in 1917.

A hall built on stilts was added to the side of the chapel in 1935. This was replaced in 1961, but the buildings were becoming life-expired. A new chapel was therefore opened in 1980. The church has prospered in recent decades and in 1976 a branch Sunday School was opened on the Chantry estate, to the south of the town. This has subsequently developed into the work at Shepherd Drive.

A few years ago the church's name was changed to avoid causing confusion among the increasingly multi-cultural local population. With this church we are a world away from some of the rural chapels in this book.

Location: 35 Cauldwell Hall Rd, IP4 4QG; OS grid ref.: TM183451

For further information

John Whinney, 'Church Profile: Mount Zion Ipswich', G June 1987, pp.5–7

www.chrbc.org.uk

Ipswich, Shepherd Drive

In the 1960s, the area to the south of Ipswich began to be developed, with large new housing estates. Suffolk Strict Baptists recognized the need for a church to be planted, and in 1976 Mount Zion took over responsibility for a Sunday School which had been started in 1972 by a member living on the Chantry estate.

A building was designed by the architect V.J. Thower, a member at Mount Zion, and opened in 1995. After a brief period from 1993 as an independent church, oversight was resumed by the church at Cauldwell Hall Road in 2005. In recent years the church has flourished, with congregations now averaging over eighty.

Location: Laburnham Close, Pinewood, IP8 3SL; OS grid ref.: TM132428

For further information

To commemorate the opening to the glory of God of Shepherd Drive Baptist Church, Ipswich on Saturday 1 July 1995 at 3 p.m.

www.sdbc.org.uk

Ipswich, Whitton

Work at Whitton began in 1904, when the church at Bethesda hired the parish room for services, but permission to use it was withdrawn after six months. By 1910 an iron room was being erected, but this was sold in 1921. During subsequent decades, considerable residential development took place off the Norwich Road in Ipswich. Bethesda again sought to develop a viable outreach work, land being acquired in 1937, but war put a stop to plans to erect a permanent building. Meanwhile a Sunday School was commenced using school premises; it quickly grew, reaching a maximum of around 300 children.

After the war, permission to put up a modular concrete building was refused, but the five years' delay meant that it became possible to build something better. A large multi-purpose building with a seating capacity of 350 was erected in 1952, designed by R.J. Cooke, a member of Bethesda who had lived in the area. The work prospered, with the Sunday School having no less than 500 children on its books in 1955. In 1969 Whitton was constituted as an independent church. Since then it has continued to prosper, although the Sunday School was down to 34 by 1977, a dramatic example of the impact on churches of changing social and religious outlooks (it has since recovered!).

Location: 209 Highfield Rd, IP1 6DH; OS grid ref.: TM144468

For further information

www.whittonbaptist.org.uk

Ipswich, Zoar

The first church in this area was planted in 1824 from Grundisburgh, and met a short distance away in Dove Yard. Its fate is unknown, but Zoar was formed by the withdrawal in 1841 of most of the members of the church then meeting in Dairy Lane. Evidently their cause was viewed sympathetically by their fellow churches, as the first chapel, in David St, was built by the Suffolk and Norfolk Home Missionary Society, and opened in 1842.

In 1851 it reported an average morning congregation of 250 in a chapel seating 500. This was much larger than the membership, which was reported in 1848 as 54. The church was part of the Suffolk and Norfolk Association from 1846 to 1849, rejoining in 1912; thereafter its highest recorded membership was 145, in 1926, perhaps a function of the opening of its new building.

The view of the interior of the old chapel (below) is interesting because of the position of the communion table, enclosed by railings and with chairs either side.

A site for the new chapel was offered in 1913 but it was not until 1925 that a replacement was opened, seating 500 and designed by Messrs Johns and Slater. Gothic had been considered for the design but rejected on grounds of cost, which had the benefit of ensuring a more contemporary outcome. Inside, there is a barrel-vaulted ceiling, and the pulpit is offset at the corner of the space at the front of the chapel which was referred to as the 'choir'. The old chapel was sold in 1926. A schoolroom was opened in 1927, and a new two-storey Sunday School building in 1954, designed by a Brethren architect, R. Woodhouse Beales, FIAA, LRIBA.

Location: St Helen's St, IP4 2LH; OS grid ref.: TM172446

For further information

Zoar Baptist Chapel, St Helen's Street, Ipswich: A Record of the Opening Services, held on Wednesday, March 18th, 1925, together with the Special Sermon preached by Pastor Philip Reynolds, Ipswich, [1925]

Zoar Baptist Sunday School, St. Helen's Street, Ipswich: A Memento of the new Sunday Schoolroom, Opened to the Glory of God on Wednesday 14 July 1954, Ipswich, 1954

www.zoarbc.org.uk

Kedington, Rehoboth

Work here appears to have begun with open air preaching by Robert Powell, who became the first pastor, and meetings were initially held in various domestic premises. Houses were certified in the village by the Strict Baptists in Bury St Edmunds in 1843 and again in 1847. Bitter persecution was experienced, which may explain why when the chapel was opened in 1850 it was named 'Rehoboth', (cf. Genesis 22, 'The Lord has made room for us').

Things would not have been helped when in 1850 John Baldwin resigned from the Bury cause after being found guilty of immoral conduct, and tried to start work in Churchgate St in Bury and at Kedington, presumably in competition with the existing work. Yet, remarkably, the 1851 Religious Census return indicated an afternoon congregation of 130 in a chapel seating 150; given the isolation of its location in the hamlet of Calford Green, a mile or two out of the village, one wonders where they all came from. In 1875, the premises were enlarged in order to provide a vestry and schoolroom.

Very little is known of the church's later history, although C.W. Banks, editor of the *Earthen Vessel*, gave it an occasional 'plug' when reporting his preaching engagements there. It was never part of any association and I suspect that it was more conservative than most of the county's causes, as may have been those at nearby Haverhill and Providence, Glemsford. Last known to be active in 1900, it was still shown on Ordnance Survey maps as late as 1951, and thereafter as 'disused'. It is now a private dwelling, visible to the right of the picture below.

Location: on the south side of Calford Green, off B1061 to Sturmer; OS grid ref.: TL698453

Kesgrave

Kesgrave is an old-established village which has seen large-scale housing development since the inter-war period. Strict Baptist interest in establishing a work here can be dated to 1922, when a mission held by the Waldringfield church was so fruitful that consideration was given to establishing a permanent work. In 1926, Philip Reynolds, pastor of Zoar, Ipswich, raised the matter and a committee was appointed by the Suffolk and Norfolk Association to research the situation. The Waldringfield church lost no time acquiring a plot of land on which to build a temporary place of worship, and this was opened in 1927. A fund for a permanent building was opened in 1936; the original chapel became a hall after its replacement (architect: R. Ferguson) was opened in 1968, and was recently demolished to make way for a new development. A church was formed in 1954.

Location: Cambridge Rd, IP5 1EW; OS grid ref.: TM211454

The first chapel appears on the leaflet above, from 1966; the second, including later extensions, is shown below

For further information

www.kesgravebaptistchurch.org.uk

Lakenheath

In Sussex and Kent there were often links between causes established by Calvinistic Independents (followers of William Huntington, the 'converted coalheaver') and those later associated with the *Gospel Standard*. They differed regarding baptism, but were agreed in espousing a strongly high Calvinistic understanding of salvation, including the rejection of any kind of evangelistic proclamation which implied a duty on the part of hearers to repent and believe. Lakenheath, however, may be the only instance of such a link in the area covered by this book. Huntington preached at various locations in and around the Fens; Jireh Chapel was opened in Back St in 1815 (now used by a Pentecostal church), and a church formed in 1819, which appears to have been Baptist. In due time, attempts were made to adopt open communion under the ministry of Edward Blackstock, and those of Strict Baptist views withdrew around 1841; this chapel was built for them in 1845. A schoolroom to the rear was added in 1903. Major renovation was undertaken to both during the 1990s.

The flint facing of the walls is unusual in this book but typical of the locality; nearby are two other chapels faced with flint, one being Jireh. Although the box pews have not survived, the well-kept interior retains its original pulpit and offers a good example of a typical Baptist chapel. The church is on the Gospel Standard list.

Location: Mill Rd, IP27 9DU; OS grid ref.: TL715828

For further information

Anon., *Lakenheath Strict Baptist Chapel, 1845-1995*, [Lakenheath, 1995]

W.S. Cooper, *'Goodness and Mercy', being the Autobiography of William Sutherden Cooper, Pastor of the Strict Baptist Chapel, Lakenheath, Suffolk, for Forty Years*, Croydon, 1943

Laxfield*

Preaching from Diss began in the village in 1797, and a church was formed in 1808 by the dismissal of members from the church at Horham, which had been founded in 1799. A room had been fitted up for worship in 1807, but increasing congregations made it necessary to replace this by converting a double cottage the following year. The chapel was built in 1810; unusually it was provided with a inside baptistery from the beginning.

From 1816 to 1821 the minister here was John Foreman, who went on to a distinguished pastorate in London. However, his successor was a minister named Latham, who adopted Unitarian views, which resulted in the dispersal of his congregation and the closure of the chapel for some years. Something similar happened with William Ward, the minister of the church at Diss, in 1822; a few years earlier other high Calvinist Baptists elsewhere in England belonging to a group known as the 'Western Schism' had also temporarily adopted non-Trinitarian views. Clearly this was a time of doctrinal ferment, and Job Hupton of Claxton had felt it necessary in 1821 to warn the churches of the old assocation against errors of this type in its annual letter.

In 1828, George Denny Spratt, then living at Fressingfield, had the chapel reopened, beginning by commencing a Sunday School. The congregation was soon built up again, and the church re-formed in 1831. Within a few years it joined (and has remained in) the new association. The chapel was enlarged in 1850 with a new schoolroom being added. The extra space would have been welcome for the 1851 Religious Census return claimed an average afternoon attendance of 890! Membership in the mid 1860s stood at 270, remarkable given the size of the village.

Not visible from the road, the chapel roof has two spans of glazed black pantiles. Certain touches mark out the building as worth attention, such as the fanlights above the doors, and the way in which two of the bays at the front are slightly recessed. Inside, six collecting boxes bear appropriate biblical texts (see the picture). The building was renovated and reseated in 1897, although most of the benches in the gallery are original, and include singers' pews with music rests. The large window in the middle dates from the renovations, at which point the pulpit was moved from the back of the present building to the front. In 1953 another hall was added at the rear.

This is the other Suffolk chapel besides Beccles which has a memorial to a local Marian martyr. John Noyes was put to death in 1557; the tablet, which was another addition during the 1897 renovations, records his dying charge.

Location: High St, IP13 8DZ; OS grid ref.: TM294724

For further information

Anon., 'A Brief History of the Baptist Church, Laxfield, Suffolk', *GH* vol. 51 (1883), pp.37–40

Anon., 'Laxfield Baptist Church', *G* February 1996, pp.12–13

[H. Bull], *One Hundred Years of Life and Light at Laxfield, Suffolk: A Centenary Souvenir, 1831–1931*, Ipswich, [1931]

Noel M. Reeve, unpublished history, 2001

www.laxfieldbaptist.org.uk

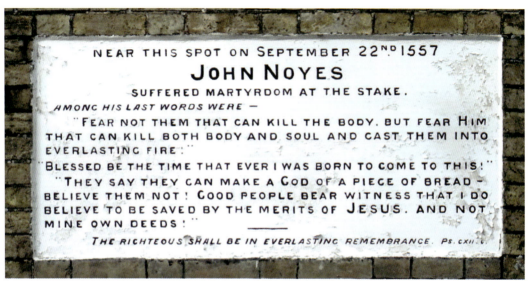

Leiston, Faith

A room in Leiston had been licensed for worship by Daniel Wilson of Tunstall as early as 1808, but nothing appears to have come of this effort. It was not until 1877 that the Aldringham church began Sunday evening services in this industrial town, using a schoolroom in Crown St until 1928, when a mission hall in Kings Road was opened. Between 1943 and 1949, the chapel was in use as a labour exchange and services had to be held elsewhere.

In 1927 a division at Aldringham resulted in the formation of a new church, 'Faith', at Leiston, by the minister, John Hallum Barker. Initially meetings were held in the Friends' Meeting House and elsewhere, but a new chapel was opened in 1928, designed by a local architect, C.H. Lay FRIBA, who had also designed the replacement chapel at Aldringham. The outreach work from Aldringham also continued.

During the war, 'Faith' was requisitioned for military use, being handed back to the congregation in 1949 after no less than nine years. The church gradually declined thereafter to just three members, but the Aldringham mission work was in a healthier state and from the mid 1960s discussions took place with the Aldringham church regarding a reconciliation. From 1973 these were sealed by a merger of the two congregations to form a new church, Leiston Baptist Church. Initially both premises were used for services but in 1976 the chapel at Aldringham was closed and the main focus of the church's work moved to Leiston, where most members lived. A new schoolroom had been built in 1967, and over the years since the work has stabilized and grown somewhat. The Kings Road premises, which had latterly been used for youth work, were sold in 1990 with planning consent for replacement by two dwellings.

Originally the whole chapel was weatherboarded in the same way as the entrance porch visible in the picture. Unusually, there is a memorial tablet on one of the gateposts, to John Hallum Barker, the founder.

Location: John St, IP16 4DR; OS grid ref.: TM445621

For further information

Anon., 'Aldringham Chapel sold', *G* July 1987, pp.8–9

John Hallum Barker, *How the Chapel was Built: A Tribute to God's Faithfulness*, Leiston, [1932]

Noel Reeve, unpublished history of Aldringham chapel, 1993

Noel Reeve, unpublished history of Leiston, Faith, 2003

www.leistonbaptist.co.uk

Records

AGBC(EA): Minutes etc, 1927–72

SRO(I): FK2/6/12–13, marriages, 1930–51

Lowestoft, Providence

A small chapel was opened in the Kirkley area of Lowestoft in 1868, and a church formed the same year. It had little or nothing to do with other Suffolk churches as it was Gospel Standard in its outlook from an early stage. Providence Chapel, a little gem of a building, was opened for it in 1878.

The Sunday School ceased in 1913 as the pastor could no longer carry it on. Minutes ceased to be kept in 1916, and it seems to have closed for a few years thereafter, possibly because the pastor wanted to move away from Lowestoft, which was felt to be a location exposed to enemy activity. Services were still being held in the 1930s, but in 1939 it had closed. After closure the chapel was used as a store. In 1981 it was reopened by a Reformed Baptist church, but they moved on and by 2005 it was being used as an office.

Location: Richmond Rd; OS grid ref.: TM543919

For further information

G January 1982

Records

SRO(L): CH169/25/18, Accounts for Charity Commissioners, 1949-54

SRO(L): NC723, Minutes, 1868-1916

Lowestoft, Tonning St

The Particular Baptist church at Lowestoft (now in London Rd but until 1852 in High St) was founded in 1813 by the church meeting at the Tabernacle, Great Yarmouth. It had been a member of the new association from 1837 to 1846, but after adopting open communion a split resulted in the formation of a new congregation in 1860. This was one of several Strict Baptist causes formed around this time and for this reason. The Tonning St chapel appears to have been built the same year, and was claimed to seat 500, but in 1870 it was reported that it had had to be repurchased and legally secured after slipping out of the control of the trustees. A few years later, it was asserted somewhat mysteriously that 'Some of its previous ministers were far from being men of angelic purity',[2] and during the 1870s membership fell from 52 to 14. All this points to an unstable cause. The chapel closed in 1887, but by 1889 the Home Mission Society committee had undertaken to reopen it as a mission station. The church was re-formed in 1894 and its application to join the Suffolk and Norfolk Association was accepted the following year. It reached 64 members by 1904 but then contracted steadily, ceasing to belong to the association around 1910, and closure followed in 1916. By 1925 the building was the home for a congregation of moderate Exclusive Brethren, and remains in Brethren use today; their tenure of the building has been more settled than that of the Strict Baptists.

Location: Tonning St, NR32 2AL; OS grid ref.: TM545930

For further information

A. Vaughan Thomas, *Centenary Souvenir of the London Road Baptist Church, Lowestoft (1813–1913)*, Lowestoft, 1913

---

[2] *EV* vol. 31 (1875), p.353.

Mendlesham Green, Jireh

In 1824 a church was formed by the dismissal of a number of members from the church at Stoke Ash. It is not clear where they met initially, but Jireh Chapel was built in 1839. The church applied to join the Suffolk and Norfolk Association in 1841/2, but it was felt that more information was needed (a reference a few years earlier in the Stoke Ash records implies that the division had not been an entirely amicable one, and the first pastor was a man who was not wanted at Stonham, where he was a member), and in the end the church was not received into the association until 1886.

Work prospered, however; in the 1851 Religious Census return the minister stated that for much of the year there was not sufficient seating for the congregation, which could be as many as 300. In the mid 1850s, therefore, the chapel was extended (at the far end in the picture above). But membership of the church had declined to 20 as early as 1914. War caused further problems: early in World War I the chapel was taken over for some weeks by the Army, and in 1949 it was reported that the chapel had been redecorated and reopened after sustaining war damage.

Thereafter work continued but the congregation was never large, and the chapel was closed in 2011 for the time being.

Location: Mendlesham Green, IP14 5RG; OS grid ref.: TM094633

As in some other chapels (e.g. Rishangles), partitions allowed upstairs rooms to double up as Sunday School classrooms and overflow accommodation for large gatherings such as anniversary services

A wall-mounted war memorial tablet in the chapel testifies to the way in which many Suffolk chapels were deeply rooted in their village context; it commemorates not only men with a chapel connection, but others living in the parish. Such a relationship with the local community has often existed in tension with the Baptist belief in a 'gathered church', of believers called out from the world to belong to Christ.

Over the inner door at the front entrance an unusual plaque commemorates the chapel's opening in 1839

Norton*

A house in the village was certified for worship in 1794, presumably from Bury St Edmunds. The present congregation was in existence by 1831, and in 1834 a local man apparently unconnected with it, named Hustler, gave a piece of ground and £100 towards a new chapel. He died the following year, leaving £100 to each of 20 needy Baptist ministers in the county.

A replacement building appears to have been erected in 1843, capable of seating 300. In 1851 it reported an afternoon congregation of 200 (membership that year was 51). The church remained in membership with the Strict Baptist association for most of the nineteenth century, but later joined the Suffolk Baptist Union.

Location: Woolpit Rd, IP31 3LU; OS grid ref.: TL957657

The doorway is unusual in commemorating the founder, although he would perhaps more correctly be described as the benefactor

Occold

The chapel (left) as it appeared during the mid twentieth century (Ralph Chambers, courtesy of SBHS), and (below) as it appears now

A church appears to have been formed and a chapel built a prominent site in the centre of the village in 1838, as the result of cottage meetings being held in the village by members of the Horham church since about 1832. The new cause joined the old association for a few years; since 1841, however, it has been in membership with the Strict Baptists.

The chapel was enlarged in 1845, resulting in an unusual duplicated frontage to the building. In 1851 it was reported that it seated 320, and saw congregations of 200 in the morning, 250 in the afternoon, and 100 in the evening. Three years later the church recorded its largest membership (96).

Inside, the chapel used to have a rather cramped gallery, but the interior was completely altered in 1994. An extension was completed in the early 1980s, but part of the chapel had to be taken down subsequently for structural reasons. Nevertheless, the building is still the home for an active congregation, Jubilee Baptist Church, formed in 2012 after the two causes which had existed in the village for twenty years were reunited.

Location: Mill Rd, IP23; OS grid ref.: TM157707

For further information

AGBC(EA): A.J. Lankester, 'Occold Strict Baptist Church', typescript, 1962

Records

AGBC(EA): Minutes, 1889–1963, etc

SRO(I): IN400/143/5, George Sherman's charity for Baptist ministers, returns, 1905–31

Otley*

Around 1796 John Thompson of Grundisburgh began preaching in Otley. In spite of opposition, the first chapel on this site was erected in 1800 and a church formed that year. A second building was registered for worship in 1802, which was enlarged, re-roofed and renovated in 1837. The present chapel does, however, include the north wall (behind the pulpit) of the smaller 1800 chapel, and it is possible to see where the original windows were located. The chapel's gault brick frontage is nicely matched in the later nineteenth-century extension to the side, and both have shuttered windows at ground-floor level, unusual for the chapels in this book.

The congregation grew rapidly and was active in several neighbouring villages. Education was seen as part of its outreach, as was the case elsewhere; in 1836 the church reported that an adult school had been commenced. 'Some in the congregation, who previously could not read, have made such progress as to be able to read easy parts of the New Testament' and the Holy Spirit had spoken to their souls as a result.[3] Even though there were other congregations nearby, congregations in 1851 were reported to average 400 in the morning, 450 in the afternoon, and 50 in the evening (plus 62 scholars morning and afternoon).

The church withdrew from the old association in 1848, disagreeing with the admission of many churches practising open communion. It did not join the Suffolk and Norfolk Association, however, until invited to do so in 1898; it withdrew in 1912 but the invitation was successfully repeated in 1921.

Otley's attraction is that it still looks like a nineteenth-century chapel. The appearance of its exterior has not been altered, and it retains a full assemblage of buildings straddling the road. Next to the

---

[3] *Circular Letter, on 'The Priesthood of Christ,' addressed by the Suffolk and Norfolk Association of Particular Baptist Churches, met at Clare, Suffolk, June the 7th and 8th, 1836* (Ipswich, 1836), p.21.

chapel is the manse, and opposite the chapel is the former stable block (partly converted in 1973 into a meeting room for the Sunday School), adjoining which is the burial ground.

Another feature of interest is provided by the benches in the gallery facing the pulpit. They are the earliest seating in the building, retained when in 1868 the interior was remodelled and the side galleries replaced. Here the Sunday School would meet before the morning and afternoon services; pupils would sit facing the superintendent's desk, and when the service began, they would turn round and face the pulpit.

Most of the rest of the pews date from the later nineteenth century; those on the ground floor have half-height doors. In 1925 the pulpit was moved back against the wall when the gallery behind it, which the choir had used, was removed; a platform was made for the choir. The stairs to the old choir gallery are still visible from the outside, at the back of the single-storey extension.

The church now has a much smaller membership than it had in its heyday, but the chapel remains open for regular worship.

Location: Chapel Rd, IP6 9NU; OS grid ref.: TM207558

For further information

Noel M. Reeve, unpublished history, 2000

Noel M. Reeve, *What God hath done: 200 Years of Gospel Witness at Otley Baptist Chapel 1800–2000*, Otley, 2000

P.B.W[oodgate]., 'The Church at Otley, Suffolk', *GH* vol. 50 (1882), pp.179–81

Records

TNA: RG4/1856, births, 1800–37

Rattlesden

Preaching in a cottage in the village took place as early as 1784, supplied by Wattisham. In 1807 Joshua Cooper, a member at Stowmarket, certified a house in the village for worship, but his church did not support this, believing that a church at Rattlesden was not required. Work therefore came under the wing of the church at Bury. A chapel was provided in 1808, the cost being met by Joshua's brother John and his wife, who lived at Drinkstone.

Above: The 1808 chapel. Below: the interior; notice the seating crammed into every available space, and the ubiquitous solid fuel stove (both courtesy of AGBC(EA))

A church was formed by the dismissal of a nucleus of members from Bury. Growth was such that in 1815 the chapel had to be enlarged; a barn in the village was also certified by a member of the Bury

church the same year. When the new association was formed in 1829, Rattlesden became a member and has remained so ever since. Over the years, the church was fortunate in that it rarely had a long period between pastors.

In 1858 the chapel was enlarged again, and in 1892 it was completely rebuilt; part of the old building was adapted to serve as a schoolroom.

The church was active in a number of the surrounding villages, but as was the case elsewhere problems could arise at times. For example, relations between the Rattlesden church and the work at Buxhall during the 1860s were sometimes difficult, but by 1902 the pastor was conducting a weekly service in the Primitive Methodist chapel, which had been built in 1875. During the twentieth century the membership declined from its peak of 118 in 1906, but the church continues to maintain a full programme of worship and outreach activities, making use of a recent extension to the side of the chapel.

Location: Felsham Rd, IP30 0SF; OS grid ref.: TL975588

For further information

SRO(B) / DWL: J. Duncan, unpublished typescript history, 1960s

H.T. Hitchcock, *Rattlesden Baptist Church 1814–1963: A Short History of the Church and its Pastors for the past 150 years*, Hadleigh, 1963

www.rattlesdenbaptistchapel.co.uk

Records

AGBC(EA): Transcript of minutes, 1813–31, etc

Rishangles, Zion*

Work began here by 1800, preachers being sent from Diss and Stowmarket. However, this eventually ceased, and a new start was made about 1840. Numbers were converted to Christ and baptized as believers, and a church was formed in 1849 by the dismissal of a nucleus of over 50 members from Grundisburgh, no less than 15 miles to the south. In the Religious Census of 1851, average attendances were reported to be 200 in the mornings and 250 in the afternoons, plus scholars; doubtless the congregation was drawn from a wide area, although there were other Baptist churches nearby at Eye, Hoxne, Horham, Stradbroke, Occold and Stoke Ash. This was a strongly Baptist area.

The present chapel replaced a clay lump building of 1841 (extended in 1848) in 1862. The gallery has removable panels and can also be used as a schoolroom. Until the building was reseated in 1986, there was a communion table set lengthwise in front of the pulpit, with pews either side and a baptistery underneath.

The communion table and pews are visible in the centre of this picture of the interior (courtesy

of Rishangles Baptist Church)

Membership peaked at 144 in 1870, but thereafter the cause (and the village) suffered severely from depopulation, and by 1908 it was down to 30 before recovering somewhat.

Recent years have seen a measure of growth. A two-storey extension to the rear was brought into use in 1993, and in 1995 the cottages to the side (which date from the 1740s) were restored and now serve as a manse. The Baptist chapel is now the only place of worship in the village, the Anglican church having been converted into a house. The church withdrew from the AGBC(EA) in 2000, and joined Partnership, a group of churches with Brethren roots.

Location: 1 Bedingfield Rd, IP23 7JZ; OS grid ref.: TM161687

For further information

John Betts, 'Church Profile: Rishangles Church … A Brief History', *G* February 1990, pp.19–21

Keith Robathan, *'The Church on the Corner': An Historical Account of Rishangles Baptist Church, Compiled following the 150th Anniversary in 1999*, [Rishangles, 1999]

G April 1993

www.rishanglesbaptistchurch.org.uk

Saxmundham

Saxmundham is one of those causes that never quite got off the ground, in spite of being located in a centre of population. The first church here was formed in 1823, with the dismissal of ten members from Aldringham, but it had probably ceased to meet by the time of the 1851 religious census as no return was included.

In 1854 a chapel was opened in Albion St, and a church formed the following year; lack of reference in contemporary reports to previous work suggests that this had ceased some while before. The chapel was purchased by the church in 1861, having probably been private property until that point. Things did not progress smoothly: references in the Halesworth church's minute book indicate that the Saxmundham church was dissolved around 1859 and re-formed in 1861. Another re-formation took place in 1901. For some years thereafter it was the base for a missioner appointed by the Home Mission Society. By the inter-war period it seems to have come under the oversight of Sudbourne, but services apparently ceased in 1932, mission services that year evidently proving unfruitful. Since being sold, the building has been adapted for use by the British Legion, with a single-storey extension at the front.

Location: Albion St; OS grid ref.: TM384631

For further information

EV vol. 11 (1855), pp.52, 119–20

Somersham

In this view, the old chapel can be seen beyond the schoolroom on the right (courtesy of AGBC(EA))

Meetings began here in 1819, several Baptist Christians having moved into the locality, and a church was formed in 1827 by the dismissal of six members from Ipswich, Stoke Green. The chapel was built in 1823 and doubled in size in 1866, with a gallery being added, and stabling a few years later. A day school was being conducted in the vestry around 1851.

The church has been in membership with the Suffolk and Norfolk Association since 1836, and its highest membership was 62, around 1870. From the early 1960s until 1996 the work was at a low ebb; for much of the time it was under the care of the association's Home Mission, with the involvement of the churches at Mt Zion, Ipswich and Great Blakenham. Safety concerns led to the use of the schoolroom (added in 1927) for worship from 1974 and the demolition of the chapel around 1983. However, recent years, and the appointment of a pastor, have seen an upsurge in its fortunes. The schoolroom became the new chapel and another ancillary building (replacing a portacabin) was erected in the 1990s on the site of the old chapel.

Location: Chapel La, IP8 4QE; OS grid ref.: TM083488

For further information

AGBC(EA): Anon., 'Short Account of the History of the Strict Baptist Church at Somersham, Suffolk, 1827–1927', manuscript, 1927

Noel M. Reeve, unpublished history, 2003

G September 1974, p.19

www.findachurch.co.uk/churches/tm/tm04/somershambc/

Southwold

Around 1810 the first Baptist service was held in Southwold, and a room was licensed for worship. A church was formed in 1821, meeting in a chapel built that year on land leased from the corporation. It was in membership with the new association for a few years from 1834, but was already struggling, and although the Home Mission Society raised funds to support a missioner, by 1836 these were no longer sufficient for him to continue. Another was appointed the following year, but ill-health forced his resignation, and by 1841 work had ceased. By 1851 services had restarted, that year's census return indicating that it seated 200 and had a congregation of 50 at the afternoon service, the best attended of the three. Trade directories in 1855 and 1858 refer to the existence of a Baptist chapel in the town. But in 1860 the trustees reached an agreement with the corporation regarding its right to resell the chapel, which implies that work had again ceased. The building still stands and is now a house. There is a stray reference (in a history of London Road, Lowestoft) to Baptist work at Southwold in 1885, but it is not clear what relation this bore to the earlier cause.

Location: Spinners Lane, off High St; OS grid ref.: TM505763

For further information

Robert Wake, *Southwold and its Vicinity, Ancient and Modern* (Yarmouth, 1839), pp.269–70

Records

SRO(L): 491/13F/23, 24; 841/7/9/4/25, documents relating to the lease granted by the corporation

Stoke Ash

The view of the chapel from this angle is virtually unchanged today (Ralph F. Chambers, courtesy of SBHS)

It is not known how Baptist work at Stoke Ash began, but the church was formed in 1805, most of the original members being dismissed from Diss. A chapel was also registered that year. It was replaced in 1846, the old chapel having become unsafe; apart from the need for increased seating accommodation, the walls were of clay lump. In the same year the church joined the new association, and has remained in membership ever since. As with several other chapels, its apparently isolated location served it well since its congregation came from several surrounding villages; the stable added in the mid 1830s would have been very useful! Nowadays it is easily missed in spite of being an imposing building, hidden by trees although only a few yards from the A140.

Average attendance as reported in 1851 was no less than 350 in the morning and 500 in the afternoon, plus 120 scholars at each service; the highest membership reported was 208, in 1864.

In 1859 the chapel and schoolroom were enlarged, and the end of the chapel rebuilt in 1869 because it had become unsafe. The front elevation is similar to that of Rishangles, with two gabled porches, and inside there is a gallery on three sides. That facing the pulpit is closed off by shutters, having been intended for Sunday School use. Box pews were removed during the 1930s. Electricity was only installed in 1963, such a delay being common in rural chapels.

Location: Chapel La (off A140), IP23 7EU; OS grid ref.: TM113713

Among the mission stations established by the church were **Thorndon**, where an attractive small mission hall was erected in 1939, and **Yaxley**, where the Congregational chapel was taken over in 1949 after it had closed. Yaxley closed in 1971 and has since been demolished. In time the work at

Thorndon passed into the hands of the Occold church, but it became increasingly intermittent and finally ceased around 1993. The building was sold shortly after and is now a private dwelling.

Location (Thorndon): The Street; OS grid ref.: TM139696

For further information

O.F. Clarke, *Stoke Ash Baptist Church 1805–1955: The Story of 150 Years*, Hadleigh, [1955]

Alfred Mowle, 'Church Profile: Stoke Ash, an Historical Perspective', *G* April 1989, p.15

Noel M. Reeve, 'Two Hundred Years in Partnership with Christ', 2005; downloadable from www.stokeashbaptist.co.uk

Noel M. Reeve, unpublished history, 2004

Thorndon mission hall

Stonham Parva, Bethel

The cause here probably had its roots in a cottage meeting, which was apparently supplied with preachers from Otley and Stowmarket. Bethel Chapel opened in 1816, the walls having timber frames on a brick base. A church was formed in 1823 with the dismissal of sixteen members from Otley. Enlargement of the building followed in 1833, when its highest membership (64) was recorded. In 1960 the cottages in front of the chapel were demolished and a car park made.

Things did not always run harmoniously for this congregation. A division around 1837, caused by problems associated with the debt outstanding on the chapel, resulted in a short-lived church being formed at nearby Earl Stonham; the Suffolk and Norfolk Association appointed a committee to arbitrate, and things appear to have been sorted out. The church was re-formed again in 1860, through the efforts of Charles Merrett, pastor at Mendlesham Green, but did not rejoin the association until 1901. The church withdrew in 1999, no longer being able to accept the basis of faith.

Location: on A140, about 100 metres south of the Magpie Inn; IP14 5JT; OS grid ref.: TM119603

For further information

H.E. Cox, *From Vision to Reality: A Short History of 'Bethel' Baptist Chapel, Stonham Parva*, Stonham, 1960

Stowmarket, Bethesda*

Work in the area seems to have commenced at Wetherden, a house being certified for worship in 1790 by a member of the church at Diss. A church was formed in 1795 (it became independent of Diss in 1797), and meetings continued in the home of William Rust, the first pastor. Baptisms took place on a farm at Battisford, several miles out of town. After Rust's death in 1797 part of his house was purchased by the church and fitted up for worship; a baptistery was installed in 1799. A purpose-built chapel was opened in 1813, a vestry being added in 1827 and the chapel enlarged and a gallery provided in 1836 (the extension is visible on the right of the picture and includes the earlier vestry). A timber-panelled gallery now runs round three sides of the chapel.

The church's history after 1818 was marked by a succession of calls to the pastorate which failed to secure united support from members; internal dissension was thus a recurrent feature. The same year which saw the enlargement of the chapel (1836) saw a division which resulted in the commencement of a work at Wetherden. All the same, in 1851 the pastor reported an average afternoon congregation of 500 plus 120 scholars.

In 1862, a second and more damaging division led to the formation of another Strict Baptist church, which met at first in the Assembly Room and then at Pilgrim Lodge, a little way along the road on the opposite side. Reconciliation took place in 1889. Extensive interior alteration and reorientation was undertaken at Bethesda in 1890, funded by the sale of Pilgrim Lodge (it was demolished in recent decades).

During World War II the chapel was requisitioned for use as a rest centre. After the war, the congregation began to grow, and a succession of alterations was made to the premises. A new entrance was provided in 1950, making the chapel visible from the road for the first time. In 1957 an organ from a Methodist chapel in Attleborough was installed, which necessitated remodelling of the pulpit, platform and choir pews. An entrance extension was added around 1962, a new hall in 1966, and further ancillary accommodation more recently. Since joining the association in 1877, the church's highest membership was 142, reached as recently as 1995.

Remarkably, the original building has no proper foundations, a fact which caused one recent pastor some concern when a bulldozer was at work in the vicinity!

Location: Bury St, IP14 1HF; OS grid ref.: TM048589

For further information

Anon., 'Church Profile: Bethesda Baptist Church, Stowmarket', *G* December 1988, pp.14–17

David Allen, *Two Hundred Years of Baptist History in Stowmarket*, [Stowmarket, 1997]

SRO(B) / DWL: John Duncan, 'The History of the Baptist Church in Stowmarket', typescript, 1966

www.stowmarketbaptistchurch.org

Records

SRO(I): FB221/A/11/1–7, deeds and other documents relating to the sale of Pilgrim Lodge to the Anglican parish, c.1890

SRO(I): FK2/3/1, register of births, 1793–1837

The Pilgrim Lodge chapel (courtesy of SBHS)

Sudbourne, Rehoboth

This church was formed in 1860, although it is not clear by whom. At first it met in an old workhouse; when the congregation outgrew it, they moved to the village blacksmith's shop. In 1863 a chapel was opened, possibly being converted from a cottage; one can understand, after the initial accommodation, why it was named 'Rehoboth'. The chapel was enlarged as early as 1866/7, a small gallery being added above the main entrance. A schoolroom was brought to the site from Clacton in 1928. Eventually it became worn out and in 1986 a replacement was built as an extension to the chapel.

The church was in membership with the Suffolk and Norfolk Association from 1865 to 1880, its membership reaching 50 in 1872. After it rejoined in 1923, membership was often below 20, and as a small cause, for some years from 1904 it was under the care of the missioner at Saxmundham.

The chapel was closed when the whole village was evacuated from 1942 to 1947, an event commemorated by a plaque on the rear wall. Members came under the care of the church at Tunstall. Before reopening, it was repaired and repainted by the Ministry of Works. Thereafter the same pastor looked after the churches at Sudbourne and Tunstall, and in 2009 they finally merged. Both chapels had recently been modernized and have been retained for regular worship.

Location: School Rd, IP12 2BE; OS grid ref.: TM414531

The interior in the early 1960s (courtesy of AGBC (EA))

For further information

Norman R. Neilson, *A Brief History of the Sudbourne Baptist Church during the first One Hundred Years*, Sudbourne, 1960

Paul Pontin, 'Sudbourne Church Hall opened', *G* July 1987, p.19

www.stbaptist.co.uk

Sudbury, Ebenezer

As early as 1790 a house had been certified for worship by John Hitchcock of Wattisham, and by 1821 a group connected with the Particular Baptist church at Sible Hedingham in Essex were meeting. The present congregation had its origins in the decision in 1850 of the Baptist church in Sudbury (which had belonged to the Strict Baptist association from its formation in 1834 until 1837) to change from strict to open communion, which resulted in division in 1851 and the formation of a Strict Baptist congregation, with the help of Rehoboth, Bury St Edmunds. Services were held in a home in Garden Row until the chapel was built in 1859. It did not join the Suffolk and Norfolk Association until 1933, but has remained in it ever since, and like many smaller causes it has been helped by that relationship. By 1991 it was being assisted by the churches at Bradfield and Hadleigh; in more recent years it has benefited from having a pastor and has begun some innovative outreach activities, such as a ladies' reading group.

Location: New St, CO10 1JB; OS grid ref.: TL872415

For further information

Anon., 'Ebenezer Baptist Church, New Street, Sudbury', G January 1997, pp.24–5

www.sudburybaptistchurch.co.uk

www.gracebaptistsudbury.co.uk

Records

SBHS: minutes, undated

Sutton

The old chapel, courtesy of AGBC(EA)

The story is told that early in the nineteenth century, a young man used to visit his girlfriend, who lived in Sutton. He was a Baptist, and persuaded a few people to gather for prayer and Bible reading. Preaching followed. Whether this has any factual basis cannot be established, but the first pastor, Samuel Squirrell, recorded that he began preaching here in 1806; many conversions and baptisms followed.

The first chapel was built by 1810, when the church was formed by the dismissal of 65 members from Grundisburgh. An inside baptistery was added in 1829. This was evidently not a wealthy congregation; in 1836 it reported: 'This church feels much of the distress which pervades the labouring class, and its poor members sometimes find it difficult to reconcile their present poverty with the fact of their actually belonging to the royal family of King Jesus; yet they have reason to be thankful'.[1] A schoolroom was added in 1843 and in 1846 the church joined the Suffolk and Norfolk Association; that year it recorded a membership of 93, a level never reached subsequently although it maintained several village stations in the Deben peninsula. A day school was commenced in 1850; this and an evening school continued until at least 1868. Average afternoon attendance as reported in 1851 was no less than 365 plus 80 scholars. Unusually, in 1865 the pulpit was replaced with a platform.

---

[1] *Circular Letter*, on 'The Priesthood of Christ,' addressed by the Suffolk and Norfolk Association of Particular Baptist Churches, met at Clare, Suffolk, June the 7th and 8th, 1836 (Ipswich, 1836), p.22.

The new chapel, before closure (John Rushbrook)

By World War I, the church was very low in numbers. In 1944 the association was asked to take oversight of the work at Sutton, and initially it was looked after by the same pastor as Tunstall. By 1950 the chapel was getting beyond repair and services were being held in the schoolroom. An article published in 1952 referred to the 'singing seats' at right angles to the pews, and to the kettle slowly boiling during the morning service to provide refreshment at lunchtime.

The congregation were able to erect a new chapel on the main road, which opened in 1952. In 1956 the cause came under the wing of Bethesda, Ipswich, and a leader was appointed. Like other chapels in the area, it benefitted from the involvement of American airmen serving on nearby bases. A measure of growth came during the 1970s and 1980s, but final decline set in. Work ceased in 1996, when its last pastor retired, and is now a dwelling. The old graveyard was finally sold in 2005.

Location: Main Rd (B1083), IP12 3DU; OS grid ref.: TM307461

For further information

AGBC(EA): Frank E. Deaves, 'Recollections', typescript, 1964

Noel M. Reeve, unpublished history, 1999

GH April 1952

Records

AGBC(EA): Minutes etc

SRO(I): FK2/2/1, births, 1802–46

Tunstall

East of the A12 is an isolated area, much of it given over to forestry plantations. The coast is just a few miles away, and it has been claimed that on the site of the Tunstall chapel there was a cave used by smugglers. John Thompson of Grundisburgh was the first Baptist to work in this area. He opened cottages for preaching at Bromeswell and Capel Green and took over one opened by the Independents at Iken in 1801. A cottage at Tunstall followed in 1803, which was converted into a meeting house. The preaching bore fruit, and on 9 May 1804 a church was formed by the dismissal of members from Grundisburgh.

As with other causes, the location of the chapel was convenient for worshippers coming from various directions. Such was the interest that a much larger replacement had to be erected as early as 1808; in the words of an early pastor, Daniel Wilson, doubtless recollecting the efforts which had to be expended in begging the money from sympathetic individuals and congregations, 'All this was the beginning of sorrows to me, which are not ended to this day'.[2] A baptistery was added in 1819, galleries in 1822, and the chapel enlarged in 1838 and 1843.

Daniel Wilson also licensed rooms for worship in Thorpe, Friston, Leiston, Dunwich and Orford. In 1809 his brother Robert was appointed as an evangelist to work in the area around Aldeburgh, and in due course this resulted in the formation of the church at Aldringham.

The church was approached to join the new association in 1831, but did not do so for another ten years, when it reported a membership of 238; it has remained in that association ever since apart from the years 1849 to 1855. Further churches were formed from Tunstall, including Cransford (1838), Saxmundham (1854) and Sudbourne (1860). By 1905 there were six village stations: Blaxhall

---

[2] Daniel Wilson, *The Life of Daniel Wilson, late Pastor of the Baptist Church, Tunstall, Suffolk* (Woodbridge, 1847–8), p.30.

(two), Boyton, Chillesford, Eyke and Iken. The chapel built at Boyton still survives. The last to close was at Blaxhall, which closed in 1972.

The work went through a low period between the two world wars, and in 1938 the association was asked to take oversight. However, it benefited from the temporary closure of the Sudbourne chapel as their pastor took care of the work at Tunstall. Since 2009 the church has been merged with that at Sudbourne, but both chapels continue in use, although the Tunstall chapel had previously had to be rebuilt, this being done within the shell of the old building. Now with a much smaller worship area but also with usefully modernized facilities, a portion of the chapel's old gallery survives in a store room located in the centre of the building.

Location: The Common (off B1078 towards Orford), IP12 2JS; OS grid ref.: TM373549

An open-air baptism at Orford in the early 1950s (courtesy of AGBC(EA))

For further information

Anon., *Tunstall Baptist Church: A Short History 1805–2005*, Tunstall, 2005

R.W. Murrell, *The History (abridged) of the Strict Baptist Church at Tunstall, in the County of Suffolk, from its Commencement in the year 1805 to its Centenary, 1905*, Woodbridge, 1905

Noel M. Reeve, unpublished history, 2004

Daniel Wilson, *The Life of Daniel Wilson, late Pastor of the Baptist Church, Tunstall, Suffolk*, Woodbridge, 1847-8

www.stbaptist.co.uk

The former chapel at Boyton, with door and window openings still visible

Waldringfield

Outreach in this area was begun by the church at Walton, near Felixstowe, and a chapel was built in 1821, to a design allowing for subsequent extension – just as well, since this was called for in 1822, 1824 and 1860! A gallery was added in 1828, primarily for the Sunday School. The chapel was located outside the village but near a crossroads, so the congregation could be drawn from a wide area. The church was formed in 1823 by dismissal of members from Walton. It joined the old association, but from 1836 became part of the new. In 1843 a baptistery was provided, baptisms in the Deben having tended to attract men who were intoxicated and liable to get into fights. The 1851 census return recorded an afternoon congregation of about 240 including children.

At some point after 1920, the chapel walls were rendered. Bomb damage made it unusable in 1940, and the church met in the village hall until 1946. Recent years have seen considerable growth. A youth hall was opened in 1989, since which an extension to the worship area has been added. Membership reached its highest level in 2007, with 128 on the roll, a figure which reflects vigorous evangelistic work and considerable housing development in nearby villages such as Martlesham.

Location: Newbourn Rd, Waldringfield Heath, IP12 4PT; OS grid ref: TM266449

For further information

Robin Percy, *All the Way: A Record of 176 Years of Witness 1823–1999 of Waldringfield Baptist Church*, Waldringfield, 1999

G November 1973

www.waldringfieldbc.org.uk

Records

SRO(I): FK2/6/14, marriages, 1974–7

Walsham-le-Willows

The chapel during demolition (courtesy of John Champion, Walsham-le-Willows Local History Group)

A chapel was opened in 1818, of which nothing is known, and a church formed by the dismissal of 29 members from Stoke Ash in 1822. In 1867 a new chapel was built nearby, in dark red brick with a slate roof; inside there was a gallery round three sides of the building.

This was a fairly prosperous cause when compared with many. In 1851 it reported afternoon congregations of almost 300 including scholars. Around 1870, it had over 90 members. Initially in membership with the old association, in 1850 it joined the Suffolk and Norfolk Association and remained a member until closure, apart from a period between 1888 and 1921.

However, by 1920 membership was down to 15, and decline continued inexorably. The chapel was well outside the village, near a stream which was liable to flood. From 1944 the work was overseen by the Wetherden church. The chapel remained open until 1948, but was sold in 1949 and demolished remarkably quickly. In spite of the fact that a trust fund for the maintenance of the work had been established in 1945, initial hopes that a smaller place of worship would be erected came to nothing, and work here ceased. Now, only a densely overgrown burial ground remains.

Records

TNA: RG4/2804, births, 1811–37

Wattisham*

Baptist work at Wattisham began early, from Bildeston (which had been founded in 1737), but in the late 1750s several members migrated from that church to a newly founded one at Woolverstone because of their unease with Bildeston's failure to maintain a clear Baptist identity. It was from Woolverstone that they were dismissed to form a new cause. A chapel was converted from a house and registered in 1763, being replaced by the present building in 1825. Its location on a bend in the road required a slight tapering of the vestibule when this was added later in the century, and both sides were tapered to match. The rear of the building is likewise tapered.

Along with Otley, this chapel is the most significant of all those featured in this book, not so much for any outstanding architecture as because of the survival of a typical Baptist ensemble – chapel, manse, separate schoolroom (built in 1868 and, like the chapel, Grade II listed) and graveyard. The chapel interior, which was refurbished and reseated around 1913–15 (some pews and tip-up seats were left at the rear of the gallery), has been sensitively preserved. The wood block flooring installed at that time replaced flagstones, which included gravestones, some of which may survive outside.

The location is, in spite of the proximity of the busy airfield, in the middle of nowhere, but this is:

> … one of those out-of-the-way Meetings built, not because there were any number of people to attend it in the place … but because it was in the very centre of a number of little gatherings for miles around. One might fancy at this very time, seeing the people driving to it on a Sunday morning, that the roads had been made on purpose for the people to drive to Meeting, and for nothing else besides.[3]

---

[3] Octoginta, *Reminiscences of the First Four Baptist Churches in Suffolk* (Norwich, 1892), p.38.

And they did; afternoon attendance in 1851 averaged 500, and membership in 1864 was 170.

Here, more than anywhere, one senses what it was like to belong to Strict Baptist churches in their heyday; only in recent years has the third Sunday service been discontinued. A founder member of the new association, it resigned in 2008, but remains firmly Strict Baptist in its faith and order.

Location: Hitcham Rd, IP7 7LD; OS grid ref: TM010520

Seating in the gallery was squeezed into every available space; here a small box pew was placed above the stair well and seats on the stairs

Another unusual survival is this framed scale of charges for the burial ground dating from 1907 (courtesy of AGBC(EA))

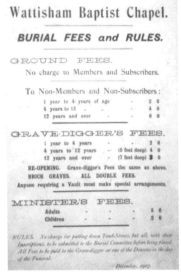

The schoolroom building stands behind the chapel

A mission chapel was built at Cross Green, **Hitcham**, in 1836, and in 1848 a day school was established at Hitcham, where a number of chapel families lived. Work in the village continued for over a century, but the chapel closed in 1965. Another mission chapel was erected at **Naughton** in 1936, but it too closed around 1965. It is now a private dwelling, and largely hidden behind a hedge.

For further information

S.K.B[land]., 'The Wattisham Church', *GH* vol. 50 (1882), pp.108–10

Records

SRO(I): register of births, 1763–1837

West Row, The Barn Chapel

One of the more unusual chapels in this book, it was converted from part of a barn during the first half of the nineteenth century. The chapel's origins are hinted at by the solidity and design of the internal supports, as well as the opening in the gable end wall. Services appear to have been held here over the twenty years to 1870 for a group who had left the Particular Baptist church in the village, but then the chapel closed, and was not reopened until 1911. The church was re-formed then, and again in 1993. This is another Gospel Standard cause.

Location: Thistley Green, West Row; OS grid ref.: TL672763

Wetherden, Providence

The old chapel; note the unusual arrangement adopted to ensure that it received sufficient light (courtesy of John Rushbrook)

Baptist work at Wetherden seems to have begun as early as 1790, when a house was certified for worship, with another following the next year. In 1821 another house was certified for worship here by a member of the church at Stowmarket. A church was founded in 1837, apparently the result of a division at Stowmarket in 1836; help was received from Cornelius Elven at Bury, and the young church joined the old association in 1838. In 1842, however, it changed allegiance to the new association, and its sympathies have remained Strict Baptist ever since.

A chapel was opened in Kate's Lane, opposite the parish church, in 1837, which appears to have been extended subsequently. Little of this building remains, apart from some evidence of the burial ground in the back garden of a cottage. Division in 1859 led to the work being overseen by Stowmarket, but it became independent again in 1870. In 1880 the church was disbanded, and by 1893 what remained of the work had come under Stowmarket once more. This time, things turned out more positively, and gradually the work became able to stand alone, returning to independence in 1918.

A new chapel, given the name 'Providence', was opened in 1927 on the edge of the village; an extensive burial ground was also provided. Oddly, neither electricity nor water were laid on for the opening, these being installed in 1934 and 1954 respectively. A garage and stable were built in 1930 for the use of those attending the services. In time additional rooms were provided at the rear of the chapel, and it has recently been extensively refurbished.

Location: Elmswell Rd, IP14 3LN; OS grid ref.: TM005629

For further information

Anon., *A Short History of the Strict Baptist Church at Wetherden, 1837 to 1937*, Wetherden, 1937

SRO(B): J. Duncan, 'The History of the Baptist Chapel at Wetherden', typescript, 1967

www.wetherdenbaptist.org.uk

Witnesham

A place of worship was registered here in 1825. The church was planted from Stoke Green, Ipswich; in 1841 it joined the Strict Baptist association, but inability to pay its dues led to its withdrawal in 1844. The present chapel was opened in 1856, and has been extended in recent decades. By 1913 it was again under the wing of Stoke Green, regaining its independence during the 1920s. The church has long been in membership with the Baptist Union.

Location: Upper St (B1077), IP6 9EW; OS grid ref.: TM183518

For further information

www.findachurch.co.uk/churches/tm/tm15/witneshambc/

Appendix 1: Membership Statistics, Suffolk and Norfolk Association

Source: circular letters / handbooks

	1831	1851	1871	1891	1911	1931	1951	1971	1991	2011
Aldringham			57	46	46	33	16	21		
Bardwell	65	81								
Beccles	131	209	152	152	80	57	58	89	94	88
Bradfield St George			83	76	59	56	43	60	90	83
Brockley							37	33	29	12
Bungay		38	73	86						
Bury St Edmunds		34								
Charsfield		105	80	49	24	31	65	30	24	15
Chelmondiston		140								
Cransford		42	51	36	34	40	35	33	14	30
Crowfield		37					40	34	46	18
Earl Soham		39								
Fressingfield			77	61	85					
Friston	31	82	70	51	35	15	9	11	18	
Glemsford, Ebenezer		148	80			18	13	12	14	
Great Ashfield		17	19							
Great Blakenham				29	59	60	41	37	47	13
Great Ellingham										38
Great Yarmouth							5			
Grundisburgh		301	262	122		69	27	25	10	16
Hadleigh	43		61	70		17	40	41	69	
Halesworth	97	55	101	51						
Horham						121	126	100	132	108
Hoxne			77	80	51		27	12	4	
Ipswich, Bethesda	91				431	602	489	712	432	
Ipswich, Mt Zion						36	52	101	99	63
Ipswich, Shepherd Dr										34
Ipswich, Whitton								37	97	114
Ipswich, Zoar						119	114	92	80	40
Kenninghall				42	27	6	11	1		
Laxfield		128	253	181	129	84	55	38	32	27
Leiston, Faith							34	10	32	26
Lowestoft, Tonning St			46							
Mendlesham Green				46	23	13	17	19	16	11
Norton		51	49							
Norwich, Gildencroft			77							
Norwich, Orford Hill			107	155	63	43	10	4		
Occold		74	64	34	37	41	31	26	19	8
Occold, Grove EC										16
Otley					96	98	77	39	18	10
Pulham St Mary			41	92	36	15	2			
Rattlesden	83		94	82	81	99	67	51	32	27	31
Rishangles			86	142	86	53	39	30	30	
Saxlingham			59							
Saxmundham				43						
Somersham			42	62	51	46	48	24	9	5	21
Stoke Ash			139	186	177	120	78	75	43	35	37
Stonham Parva	54		44			42	20	22	21	36
Stowmarket					81	73	63	54	58	119	82
Sudbourne				51			15	16	19	22	in T'stall
Sudbury								13	17	5	9
Sutton			85	64	31	13	9	10	13	14	
Tunstall				167	110	100	30	23	16	21	31
Waldringfield			87	103	46	39	79	75	31	40	118
Walsham le Willows			72	93		13				
Wattisham	138	147	162	102	67	73	65	63	55	
Wetherden		29				63	42	72	73	52
Wortwell						5				

APPENDIX 2: STRICT BAPTIST PLACES OF WORSHIP

NORFOLK

Locations underlined are where a building was still extant when I visited (2005 onwards). Gospel Standard causes are printed in bold, mission stations in italic. Postcodes are given (when known) where a building is used for worship or is accessible to the public. The 1851 census volumes are listed in the bibliography.

Location	Name & address; OS grid ref	1851 census vols ref	In S&N Assoc.	church formed in/moved to this location - closed	chapel built	notes
Alburgh				1819–fl.1822		*from Wortwell*
<u>Attleborough</u>	Leys La, NR17 2HX; TM045949	795		1820–o	(1) 1832 (2) 1979	(1) from Diss OR Ellingham & Kenninghall; dem.1960; graves remain
Aylsham				*fl.c.1880*		**supplied from Zoar, Norwich**
Banham	(1) ?Banham La (2) ?			fl.1833–fl.1892	(2) 1890s	*from Kenninghall; iron chapel built 1890s*
Banham	Banham Rd			1872-5	1872	*split from Old Buckenham; registration. cancelled 1882; chapel extant 1940s*
Banham	cottage			1907–?		*from Kenninghall*
Billingford				fl.1868		*from Hoxne*
<u>Blofield</u>	North St, NR13 4RQ, TG334096	548		1847–by 1895	1810	*from Salhouse; preaching from Zoar, Norwich c.1880* *chapel ex-Methodist; later reading room*
Bressingham		761		fl.1851	?	*part building used; possibly same as later work*
Bressingham	(1) house (2) chapel, Common Rd			1859–fl.1942	(1) 1858? (2) 1859	*under Shelfanger; under Diss by 1881 and onwards*
Brockdish	Free Methodist chapel			1933–?	1860	*from Fressingfield; later workshop & cottage*
<u>Brooke</u>	50 High Green, NR15 1JA; TM281987	631		1841–o	1841	*built with bricks from chapel at Kirstead*
Bunwell Low Common				1889–fl.1927	1889	*from Carleton Rode*
Burgh St Peter				mid 19th c.		*from Beccles*
Burston		682		fl.1851		*from Shelfanger; not used exclusively for worship*

Place	Address				Notes
Carleton Rode	6 Chapel Rd, NR16 1RN; TM118930	737	1861-3	1812-o	1812	from Gt Ellingham 1774; 1811-12 branch of Diss
Claxton	Folly La; TG337028	624	1831-8	c.1750-1943	1750s, reb. 1790s, mid 19th c.	remnant from Beccles; now dwelling; restored 1994; Claxton Opera
Claxton	***Mr Durrant's room***					***from Zoar, Norwich?***
Deopham				*fl.1870*		*from Gt Ellingham*
				fl.1851		
Downham Market, Zion	47 Priory Rd, PE38 9UJ; TF609031	1272		?-1953	1849, alt. 1874	
East Harling	chapel			1833-by 1841	1833	in 1845 directory; fl.1883 as preaching station under Kenninghall
Fersfield				*fl.1841*		*from Kenninghall*
Framingham Pigot	Chapel La; TG282037	530	1831-9	1808-fl.1867 1895-? 1902-?	1808	now dwelling *from Claxton* *from Norwich, Providence*
Geldeston				*mid 19th c.*		*from Beccles*
Gillingham				*mid 19th c.*		*from Beccles*
Gillingham	*village hall / 1982 school*			1980-5		*from Beccles; continued by local Christians*
Great Ellingham	Long St, NR17 1LN; TM019965	800	1981-8 1995-	1699-o	(1) 18th c. (2) 1824, alt.1847, 1884	
Great Yarmouth, Salem	(1) Zoar, Bank Paved Row (2) Albion Rd (3) York Rd; TG528072	17	1862-79 1949-66	1841-1966	(1) by 1845 (2) 1853 (3) 1874	split from Tabernacle 1841 (3) sold 1968; became Elim church; now flats
Haddiscoe				*mid 19th c.*		*from Beccles*
Hales				*mid 19th c.*		*from Beccles*
Harleston	Independent Chapel, Chapel Yard; TM245833	647		1846-fl.1892		from Pulham St Mary
Harleston				1982-fl.1985		*from Fressingfield*
Hempnall, Zion	*room from warehouse*	706		1848-fl.1851 1879-fl.1883	1848	*from Saxlingham*
Honing or Horning				**1877-?**		***c.1880 sometimes supplied by Zoar, Norwich***

Place	Address				Notes
Kenninghall, Bethezel	Church St		1824-30	1825	split from Zion
Kenninghall, Zion	Church St; TM040861	787	1846-9 1891-1971	1807, alt.1832, 1874	from Shelfanger later a pottery / museum
Kings Lynn, Zion	Blackfriars Rd	1216	1832-by 1907	1836	split from Broad St c.1880 supplied by Zoar, Norwich later mission hall, then Spiritualist
Loddon			mid 19th c.		from Beccles
Martham?	White St	41		(1) 1799 (2) 1879	not clear that this was Strict Baptist
Mulbarton			fl.c.1880		c.1880 sometimes supplied by Zoar, Norwich
Needham			1912-fl.1913		from Pulham St Mary
North Green			fl.1898		from Pulham St Mary, in summer
Norton Subcourse			fl.1830s		from Beccles
Norwich, Gildencroft	Gildencroft, Magdalen St; TG227093		1862-80 1860-1915	1699	split from St Marys after 1915 under St Mary's, closed 1939; virtually dem. 1942, reb.1958, burnt 1990
Norwich, Jireh	(1) room, Bedford St (2) Dereham Rd (3) room, Pottergate St		1840-9 1865-6	(1) 1830s (2) 1840 (3) c.1866	work began late 1830s (2) became 2 houses, standing 1948 (3) once used by Wesleyans merged with Providence c.1870
Norwich, Orford Hill	Orford Hill [Timberhill], NR1 3LA; TG231083	404	1868-1975	conv.1833, enl. 1838	possibly split from St Mary's merged with Salhouse
Norwich, Providence	Providence, Pitt St [Cherry La]	374	(1) 1814-fl.1875 (2) 1879-86 (3) 1898-1934	1769, alt.1818	was Calvinistic Methodist (2) from Tabernacle, to Zoar (3) from Orford Hill, merged with Zoar 1934; dem. 1936/7
Norwich, Tabernacle	St Martin-at-Palace Plain		1875-9	1755/84	built for Countess of Huntingdon to Providence, then Zoar garage / timber store; dem. 1953
Norwich, Zoar	St Mary's Plain. NR3 3AF; TG228091		1875-o	1886, alt.1946	schism c.1871 from union of Jireh and Providence; previously in Tabernacle, then Providence

Place	Location	No.	1900-c.1906	Dates	Notes
Norwich, Gordon Hall	Duke St				short lived schism from Zoar
Old Buckenham	Abbey Rd; TM066917	743	1855-1991	(1) 1831/2 (2) 1857, alt.1883	from Attleborough; under Diss 1855-9
Pulham St Mary	Station Rd, South Green; TM206843	697	1841-1952	1843, alt.1868, 1895	divided 1887-92, then re-formed; later engineer's workshop and factory previously preaching from Wortwell 1820
Rushall			fl.1898		from Pulham St Mary, in summer
Salhouse, Zion	Chapel Loke, NR13 6RA; TG314147	345	1801-o	1803, alt.1828	under Norwich, Orford Hill 1960-75
Salhouse, Rehoboth	Rehoboth, Upper St; TG317150	346	1846-fl.1864	1842	schism from Zion 1841
Salhouse, Horse Shoe Chapel		341	1853-?	fl.1851	possibly GS
Saxlingham Thorpe	(1) ? (2) Windy La; TM216978	520	1847-52 1802-1947	(2) 1821	from St Mary's, Norwich (2) sold 1955, now dwelling
Shelfanger	Common Rd; TG106840	754	1882-? 1762-1968	(1) 1768 (2) 1821	1968 with Kenninghall now dwelling
Southery	Churchgate St, PE38 0ND; TL622946	1274	1900-?, 2001-o	1845	
South Lopham	Low Common; TM058807	767	(1) 1857-76 (2) fl.1885 (3) 1892-? (4) 1899-fl.1905	1851r, alt.1868/74	(1) from Kenninghall, work began c.1850 (2)-(3) from Shelfanger (4) from Shelfanger, by 1902 Kenninghall by 1912 Brethren; now house
Swaffham			fl.1935		
Tips End, Zion	(1) Welney (2) Zion, Lakesend Rd; TL509951	1299	fl.1845-c.1983	(1) 1845 (2) reg.1874	latterly under March de-reg. 2000
Tivetshall	barn		fl.1832-by 1885		
Toft Monks			fl.1830s		from Beccles
Wortwell, Providence	Low Rd; TM274843	654	1819-1919 1929-1944	1822	from Diss, work from 1817 reopened 1924 by S&N Association chapel to RCs; now dwelling

144

SUFFOLK

Place	Location	No.	Dates	Dates	Notes
Aldeburgh	70 High St; TM464564			1823, reb.1878	from Aldringham; revived 1896/7 later used by builder
Aldringham, Providence	off Thorpeness Rd (B1353); TM457609	A2	1840-5 1862-1972	1812-1972	from Tunstall merged with Leiston 1972; mission to 1976
Ashbocking				(1) 1812 (2) 1915	from Otley
Badingham			fl.1860s-fl.1888		from Cransford
Badingham	Primitive Methodist chapel, High Rd (A1120); TM327682	462	fl.c.1904 1948-88	1836	from Laxfield; later also Cransford earlier work from Cransford fl.1904
Badwell [Ash]			fl.1857-fl.1860		from Walsham-le-Willows
Barham			fl.1902		from Gt Blakenham
Bardwell, Zion	Low St; TL940728	211	1830-53 1825-2003	1824	from Bury; house cert. 1822 closed 2003; now dwelling
Barrow, Cave Adullam	The Street; TL764635	184	c.1995-o	reg.1837	formerly Congregational; from Lakenheath
Battisford	house		fl.1860 fl.1911-1924		from Wattisham
Beccles, Martyrs' Memorial	(1) The Cockpit, New Market (2) Fair Close (3) Station Rd, NR34 9QJ; TM424905	869	1829-	(1) 1803? (2) 1805 (3) 1861	from Independents, baptized at Claxton
Beccles, Thelton Est.			1948/9?-?		from Beccles; FoY class started 1948/9
Beyton	house, Beyton Green	326	1847-fl.1851		from Bradfield
Blakenham			fl.1902		from Gt Blakenham
Blaxhall	later Village Hall		1927-? 1936 1955-72		from Tunstall
Blaxhall Common			fl.1905		from Tunstall
Blaxhall Square			fl.1905		from Tunstall
Boyton	Baptist chapel; TM380474		fl.1873 fl.1882-1917		from Sutton 1873, later Tunstall now garage

Place	Address/details	No.	Date range	Date(s)	Notes
Bradfield St George	(1) behind house, Freewood St (2) (3) Kingshall St, Rougham, IP30 9LG; TL917607	163	1866-	1844-o	(1) 1835 (2) 1850 (3) 1980	from Bury house registered 1834 in SBU by 1861 until 1866
Brandeston	(1) barn (2) Independent Chapel, The Street; TM245608	688		(1) c.1840 (2) 1850-?	(2) 1838	from Earl Soham (2) later house
Brettenham	TL964536			fl.1945-fl.1965		from Rattlesden; now house
Bricett	houses	514		1813-fl.1860	reg.1813 reg.1834	from Wattisham
Brockford				fl.1850s		from Mendlesham
Brockley Green	Chapel La, IP29 4AS; TL824545	175	1931-	1841-o	1833	plant from Bury (houses registered 1809, 1833)
Bromeswell				1852-?		from Sutton
Bruisyard	Baptist Room, Red House	740		fl.1832-fl.1851	reg.1832	from Cransford; use not exclusive
Bruisyard	canteen			fl.1955-1969/70		from Cransford; monthly
Bungay				1823-?		from Beccles, apparently gone by mid 1840s
Bungay, Bethesda	(1) Corn Exchange, Broad St (2) Chaucer St (was Neatgate St); TM335898	852-3	1849-1900/1	1846-1966	(2) 1851	from Beccles
Bungay	Baptist Room, Broad St	854		fl.1851		from Bungay; schoolroom
Bungay				**fl.1862-c.1908**		**from Zoar, Norwich**
Bury St Edmunds, Rehoboth	16 Westgate St (Out Westgate); TL852637	A13	1838-51 1896 1931-51	1838-? 1877-1952	1840	split from Garland St now offices
Bury St Edmunds, Moreton Hall	The Self Centre, Kempson Way, IP32 7AR; TL873637			2012-		from Bradfield as branch congregation
Buxhall	Primitive Methodist Chapel, Mill Green; TL996577			1860s-fl.1912	1875	from Rattlesden; chapel used by 1902
Carlton Colville				fl.1830s		from Beccles
Cavendish				1859-fl.1872		from Clare & Glemsford (2)
Charsfield	The Street; TM258563	676, 677	1849-	1809-o	1808, ext.1846	from Grundisburgh

146

Place	Location	No.	Dates	Date info	Notes
Chelmondiston	Pin Mill Rd, IP9 1JE; TL206373	565	1845-58 2011-o	1825-2006 conv.1825, reb.1854	from Ipswich, Stoke Green re-plant by Grace Baptist Partnership
Chillesford				1921-fl.1927	from Tunstall
Clare	(1) Cavendish La (2) Cavendish Rd, CO10 8NY; TL769455	46	1859-68	1803-o	(1) c.1803, reb.1821 (2) 1859	from Independents; now BU
Claydon				fl.1902	from Gt Blakenham
Combs	house			1939-by 1942	from Stowmarket
Cotton				fl.1850s	from Mendlesham
Cransford	IP13 9NZ; TM318647	738	1839-	1838-o	(1) 1841 (2) 1990	from Tunstall (2) after old one destroyed by hurricane 1987
Crowfield, Bethesda	(1) house (2) meeting house (3) Stone St, IP6 9SZ; TM149570	480	1844-55 1949-	1835-o	(1) reg.1823 (2) reg.1824 (3) 1834, enl.1835	from Ipswich, Stoke Green
Culpho?				19th c.	from Grundisburgh
Debenham				fl.1850s	from Mendlesham
Drinkstone				1813-fl.1865 fl.1900/01	from Rattlesden
Earl Soham	(1) 'Black Chapel', Little Green; TM231630 (2) Low Rd; TM229631	685	1840-63	1821-o	(1) 1821 (2) 1859	from Horham (2) closed 2009 and congregation moved to Framlingham; both now houses
Earl Stonham				1837-by 1851	schism from Stonham Parva
East Bergholt				1826-? 1858-fl.1862	from Grundisburgh later services in a cottage; chapel anticipated
Eastbridge				fl.1840s	from Aldringham
Eyke				fl.1835	from Tunstall
Eyke	converted carpenter's shop			1880-1938	from Tunstall; by 1923 also from Sutton
Felsham		344		1815 1817-fl.1851 fl.1883	(1) 1815 (2) c.1838	(1) barn reg. from Bury (2) from Rattlesden; building conv. c.1838
Foxhall				1923-?	from Waldringfield

Place		Address/Location	Dates	Dates 2	Notes
Framlingham		*Corn Exchange*		1869/70-?	*from Cransford*
Framlingham				1884-90	*from Laxfield; church formed 1890/1*
Framsden		*room*		fl.1876	*from Otley*
Fressingfield		(1) barn, Church Farm (2) Low Rd, IP21 5PE; TM263774	449	1857-1927	1839-o	(1) conv.1819 (2) 1835	from Wortwell?
Friston		(1) ? (2) Hexagon Baptist Chapel, Mill Rd, IP17 1PH; TM411601	725	1831-2009	1829-o	(2) 1831, reg.1834	from Aldringham
Glemsford, Ebenezer		Egremont St; TL828475	92	1842-52, 1859-71, 1923-92	1830-1992	1829; closed 1988	from Bury now a dwelling
Glemsford, Providence		Hunt's Hill; TL829479		1859-1965	1859	demolished by 1977
Gosbeck		TM164560		1950-89	1953	*from Crowfield*
Great Ashfield, Bethel		TM006679	311	1849-73	1848?-fl.1889	1848	work from Wetherden began c.1843
Great Blakenham		(1) two cottages (2) Chapel La, IP6 0JJ; TM126501		1889-	1876-o	(2) 1873
Great Finborough					1981-fl.1983		*from Wattisham*
Great Glemham					1907/8-?		*from Cransford*
Grundisburgh		(1) adjoining Stephen Lawrence's house (2) Chapel La, IP13 6TS; TM227502	618	1832-1907 1921-	1798-o	(1) 1796/7 (2) 1798	from Ipswich, Stoke Green
Hadleigh		George St, IP7 5BD; TM028426	138	1829-48 1852-1905 1926-2008	1815-48 1851-o	(1) 1818 (2) 1830	from Wattisham
Hadleigh Heath			143	1962-5	1823-1966	(1) 1823 (2) 1849/65, enl.1871	(1) = barn conversion

Place	Location	No.	Dates	Dates	Notes
Halesworth	(1) Loampit La; TM393778 (2) Chediston St	798	1829-1907	1819-c.1914	(1) reg.1820 (2) conv. c.1836	from Aldringham (1) now Kentread House; see Holton
Haverhill	Upper Downs Slade, CB9 8HF; TL670456	16		1828-o	1828	from Sible Hedingham
Hawstead				fl.1947/8-fl.1967	1923	from Brockley; dem. c.1989
Henley				fl.1894		from Great Blakenham work from Stoke Green fl.1865
Hessett	house			1814-?		from Bury
Hessett	house			1835-?		from Bradfield
Hessett	(1) Village Hall (2) Mission Hall, opposite Malting Farm			1890-fl.1912 1924-? fl.mid 1930s	(2) 1894	from Bradfield (2) converted from malting reopened 1924 after renovation; dem.1955
Heveningham				fl.1956-c.1960		from Laxfield
Hitcham	chapel, Cross Green; TL989529	111		1836-fl.1965	1836	from Wattisham
Hitcham	(1) cottage (2) Iron Cottage			fl.1903	(1) ?-1903 (2) 1903-?	from Wattisham
Holton	chapel	805		fl.1851-fl.1861	1820	from Halesworth
Horham	Chapel La, IP21 5ER; TM219715	454	1922-	1799-o	(1) reg.1799 (2) 1859	plant from Diss
Hoxne	(1) house (2) (3) Cross St; TM184761	436	1859-1927 1935-2002	1843-2002	(2) 1834 (3) 1865	(3) probably a rebuild of (2)
Hundon	chapel	4		1851-? fl.1905	1846	from Clare; joint with Independents from Tunstall
Iken				1824-?		from Grundisburgh by 1930s a warehouse
Ipswich, Providence	Dove Yard, St Helen's					
Ipswich, Bethesda	(1) Long La (2) Dairy La (3) Fonnereau Rd, IP4 2BB; TM165449	604	1831-42 1892-2000	1829-o	(2) conv.1792 reg.1838 (3) 1913	from Ipswich, Stoke Green (1) formerly Wesleyan (2) built for Countess of Huntingdon
Ipswich, Zoar	(1) David St (2) St Helens St, IP4 2LH; TM172446	597	1846-9 1912-	1841-o	(1) 1842 (2) 1925	secession from Ipswich, Dairy La

Place	Address	Seats	Dates	Notes
Ipswich, Mt Zion	(1) Cave Adullam, Cauldwell Hall Rd (2) (3) 35 Cauldwell Hall Rd, IP4 4QG; TM183451		1923- (2) 1912 (3) 1980	work began 1894
Ipswich, Whitton	209 Highfield Rd, IP1 6DH; TM144468		1969- 1969-o	from Bethesda; work from 1905
Ipswich, Shepherd Drive	Laburnham Close, Pinewood, IP8 3SL; TM132428		1993- 1993-o 1952 1995	from Mt Zion
Ixworth			1843-?	*from Bardwell*
Kedington Rehoboth	Kedington Hamlet (S side of Calford Green, off B1061); TL698453	21	1846-fl.1900 1850, enl.1875	
Kesgrave	Cambridge Rd, IP5 1EW; TM211454		1955- 1954-o (1) 1927 (2) 1968	from Waldringfield
Knodishall	*chapel. Colfair Green*	751	*fl.1850–fl.1851* *1852-?* *conv.1850*	*former granary; from Friston from Sutton*
Lakenheath	**Mill La, IP27 9DU TL717827**	**262**	**1845-o** **1845**	**church formed by secession from Jireh**
Laxfield	High St, IP13 8DZ; TM294724	451	1835-47 1848- 1808-22 1831-o	from Horham
Leiston, Faith	John St, IP16 4DR; TM445621		1949- 1927-o 1928	split from Aldringham
Leiston	(1) schoolroom, Crown St (2) Kings Rd		*1877-c.1990* (1) 1877 (2) 1928	*from Aldringham*
Lindsey			*fl.1830–fl.1865*	*from Wattisham*
Lowestoft			*fl.1830s*	*from Beccles*
Lowestoft	(1) High St (2) Arcade (3) London Rd		1837-46 1813-o (1) 1813 (2) 1852 (3) 1898	from Great Yarmouth, Tabernacle
Lowestoft	Tonning St, NR32 2AL; TM545930		1861-80 1895-1910 1860-87 1894-1916 1860	schism from older cause; chapel to Exclusive Brethren
Lowestoft, Providence	**Richmond Rd; TM543919**		**1868-fl.1930s** **1878**	**reopened by Reformed Baptists 1981; later builder's office**
Martlesham			*1923-?*	*from Waldringfield*

150

Place	Location/Address	No.	Dates	Dates 2	Notes
Mellis	house	411			*from Stoke Ash*
Mendlesham Green, Ireh	IP14 5RG; TM094633	377	1886-2011	1839, enl.1850s	from Stoke Ash
Mettingham					*from Beccles*
Monewden			mid 19th c.		*from Charsfield*
Naughton			fl.1894		
Newbourn	chapel		1936-fl.1965	1936	*from Wattisham; sold 1972/3; now house*
			fl.1930s?		*from Waldringfield*
Norton	Woolpit Rd, IP31 3LU; TL957657	319	1833-85, 1895-7	1831-o	(1) 1834 (2) 1843
Occold	Jubilee Baptist Church, Mill Rd, IP23; TM157707	419	1841-	1838-o	1838 *from Horham*
Occold, Grove Evangelical	Village Hall		1996- 2012	1990-2012	*division, later reconciled*
Offton	house			fl.1860	*from Wattisham*
Offton				fl.1949-fl.1956	*from Somersham*
Orford				fl.1950	*from Sudbourne rooms previously licensed by D Wilson 1808 for 18 months, 1823, 1825–fl.1829*
Otley	Chapel Rd, IP6 9NU; TM207558	614	1898-1912 1921-	1800-o	(1) 1800 (2) reg.1802, enl.1837 *from Grundisburgh*
Oulton Broad				fl.1830s	*from Beccles*
Parham	railway station waiting room, The Street; TM307606			1948-fl.1976	*from Cransford; extended to Hacheston 1969/70*
Playford	Parish Rm			1904-?	*from Grundisburgh*
Ramsholt				1854-?	*from Sutton*
Rattlesden	(1) Pantiles, Hightown Green? (2) (3) Felsham Rd, IP30 0SF; TL975588	341	1829-	1813-o	(1) house (2) 1808, enl.1815, 1858 (3) 1892 *from Bury*
Rattlesden	by 1851 Moor's Cottage, Hightown Green	340		1780s–fl.1897	*from Rattlesden*

Location	Address	No.	Dates	Year	Notes
Reading Green, nr Hoxne	Mr Harper's barn			fl.1868	from Hoxne
Rede	Mission Hall; TL805558			fl.1911-1984	from Brockley; S Sch reopened 1949
Ringsfield				mid 19th c.	from Beccles
Ringshall	house			1834-?	from Wattisham
Ringshall				fl.1905/6-fl.1912	from Somersham
Rishangles, Zion	1 Bedingfield Rd, IP23 7JZ; TM161687	382	1849-2000	1849-o	work 1799/1800 from Diss/Stowmarket; restarted, under Grundisburgh 1847-9 now Partnership UK
Rougham				fl.1847-50	from Bury, Rehoboth house certified by Bradfield 1847
Saxmundham	Albion St; TM384631		1860-76	(1) 1841, ext.1848 (2) 1862	from Aldringham now British Legion
Shottisham				1854	
Sicklesmere	room			1823-? 1855-by 1901 1901-32	from Sutton
Somersham	Chapel La, IP8 4QE; TM083488	520	1836-	fl.1923-fl.1927 1857-?	from both Bury churches
Southwold	(1) room (2) Spinners La; TM505763	824	1834-40	(1) 1823, enl.1866 (2) 1927	from Ipswich, Stoke Green
Stanstead				1821-41 fl.1851-c.1858 fl.1885?	(2) now house
Stoke Ash	Chapel La, IP23 7EU; TM114713	415	1846-	1829-by 1851	from Bury, then Glemsford
				(1) 1805 (2) 1846, enl.1859	mainly from Diss
Stoke by Clare	chapel	49		fl.1844 as joint-fl.1897	house cert. from Bury 1827 chapel shared with Baptists by 1844; reg.1817 as Independent from Clare; but Clare history states began 1853, reopened post-1920, closed 1978
Stonham Parva, Bethel	A140, IP14 5JT; TM118603	504	1829-39 1841-52 1901-99	1823-fl.1852 1860-o	1816 from Otley

Location	Address	No.	Dates	Other dates	Notes
Stowmarket, Bethesda	Bury St, IP14 1HF; TM048589	362, 363	1877-	(1) 1796 (2) 1813	from Diss
Stowmarket, Pilgrim Lodge	Bury St		1862-89	1862	split
Sudbourne, Rehoboth	(1) former workhouse (2) blacksmith's shop (3) School Rd, IP12 2BE; TM414531		1865-81 1923-2009 1948-o	(3) 1863, enl.1867	merged with Tunstall 2009
Sudbury	Church St	67	1834-7	1834-o	(1) 1834 (2) 1889	from Wattisham / Sible Hedingham now BU
Sudbury, Ebenezer	New St, CO10 1JB; TL872415		1933-	1851-o	1859	from Bury
Sutton	Main Rd; TM307461	648	1846-1996	1810-1996	(1) 1810, ext.1843 (2) 1952	from Grundisburgh
Swilland				fl.1960 -fl.1966		from Otley
Sylcham				fl.1868		from Hoxne
Thorndon		417		fl.1851		from Stoke Ash & later also Rishangles
Thorndon	The Street; TM139696			fl.1938-fl.1993	1939	from Stoke Ash (+ Occold 1981); now dwelling
Thorpeness				1903-fl.1905		reopening; from Aldringham room previously licensed by D Wilson c.1808
Tunstall	The Common, IP12 2JS; TM372549	712	1841-9 1855-	1804-o	(1) conv.1803 (2) 1808, enl.1838	from Grundisburgh
Waldringfield	Newbourn Rd, Waldringfield Heath, IP12 4PT; TM267449	645	1836-	1823-o	1821, enl.1822, 1824, 1860	from Walton
Walsham-le-Willows	Cranmer Green = Finningham Rd	305	1850-88 1921-48	1822-1948	(1) 1818 (2) 1867	from Stoke Ash
Wangford	chapel, Norfolk Rd			1831-by 1900	1831	from Southwold?
Wattisham	Hitcham Rd, IP7 7LD; TM010520	109	1829-2008	1763-o	(1) conv. 1763 (2) 1825	from Woolverstone
West Row, The Barn Chapel	**Thistley Green; TL670763**			1911-? 1993-o	**c.1850**	
Westhall				mid 19th c.		from Beccles

Location	Name/Description	No.	Date range	Date	Notes
Wetherden, Providence	(1) Kate's La (2) Elmswell Rd, IP14 3LN; TM005629	337	1842-59 1919-	(1) 1837 (2) 1927	from Stowmarket
Whepstead	cottage		1837-80 1918-o		
Wickham Skeith	house?	388	fl.1943		from Brockley
Winston	Cave Adullam		fl.1851	c.1818	from Stoke Ash
Withersdale			fl.mid 19th c.-fl.1862 1979-?		from Crowfield from Fressingfield
Witnesham	Upper St, IP6 9EW; TM183518	612	1841-4	(1) reg.1825 (2) 1856	from Ipswich, Stoke Green now BU
Woodbridge	Beaumont Chapel, Chapel St; TM271492		fl.1899	1810, enl.1841	from Grundisburgh; BU church formed 1900 now dwelling
Woodbridge	chapel, Drybridge Hill	664	fl.1842-fl.1851	reg.1820	from Grundisburgh & Waldringfield; work began 1820, church formed by 1842
Woolpit	Baptist cottage, Woolpit Heath	334	fl.1851		from Wetherden
Woolpit	cottage	A52	fl.1851		from Wetherden but no return
Woolpit			1860s-fl.1890s		from Rattlesden
Worlingham			fl.1830s		from Beccles
Worlingworth	hut		1950/1-fl.1983		from Horham; Sunday School began in garage
Wrentham			fl.1830s		from Beccles
Wyverstone			fl.1843		from Wetherden
Yaxley	Little Baptist Chapel Cong'l Chapel, Mellis Rd	428	fl.1851-fl.1899 1949-71	1826	from Stoke Ash; possibly built as Independent; chapel hired from Suffolk Congregational Union

Bibliography

Items relating to particular chapels appear on the appropriate pages. Those listed here are of more general relevance.

Unpublished

Hove, Gospel Standard Library: K.W.H. Howard, Index of Strict Baptist churches

NRO: MSS 4259-61, Maurice F. Hewett, 'Collection of material in preparation for an Historical Record of the Baptists of Norfolk and their Churches', 3 vols, typescript, [1942-7]

NRO: COL/8/83, Thomas Harmer, 'Historical & Biographical Accounts of the Dissenting Churches in the Counties of Norfolk & Suffolk', ms

NRO: COL/8/84, 85, 'Norfolk & Suffolk Dissenting Church history', 2 vols, ms notes, cuttings etc

SBHS: Ralph F. Chambers, 'The Strict Baptist Chapels of England, Volume –: The Chapels of East Anglia: Covering the Counties of Suffolk, Norfolk, and Cambridgeshire', typescript, n.d.

SRO(B): FK2/500/1/1-4, SBU minute books 1846-1960, reports to 1933

SRO(B): [Bury] Nonconformist Churches, box file

SRO(B): John Duncan, 'The History of the Baptist Church in Bury St Edmunds (The first 80 Years)', typescript, 1963

SRO(B): John Duncan, 'Suffolk Free Church History, I: 1957-64'; 'II: 1964-1968'; 'III: 1961-1969', typescript, n.d.

SRO(I): HD1842/1-11: Oswald Job, Free Church notes (1941-84), scrapbooks containing cuttings of his newspaper columns

Noel M. Reeve, unpublished histories of a number of chapels, typescript, 1993 onwards

Published

S.K. Bland, *Memorials of George Wright*, London, 1873

John Browne, *History of Congregationalism and Memorials of the Churches in Norfolk and Suffolk*, London, 1877

[A.K. Cowell], *A Short Biographical Account of the late Mr. John Thomson [sic], Many Years Pastor of the Baptist Church, Grundisburgh, Suffolk, comprising an Account of the Riots and Persecution attending the Introduction of the Gospel into Wickham-Market, In the Year 1810*, Ipswich, 1827

Kenneth Dix, *Strict and Particular: English Strict and Particular Baptists in the Nineteenth Century*, Didcot, 2001

Janet Ede & Norma Virgoe (eds), *Census of Religious Worship of 1851*, Norfolk Record Society 72, Norwich, 1998

Charles Boardman Jewson, *The Baptists in Norfolk*, London, 1957

Ashley J. Klaiber, *The Story of the Suffolk Baptists*, London, [1931]

Octoginta, *Reminiscences of the First Four Baptist Churches in Suffolk*, Norwich, 1892

Robert W. Oliver, *History of the English Calvinistic Baptists 1771-1892*, Edinburgh, 2006

Alan Rayner, *The Hills of Zion: A Pictorial History*, Luton, [2000]

Vincent B. Redstone, *Records of Protestant Dissenters in Suffolk*, Woodbridge, 1912

Philip Reynolds, *Our Position, Authority and Mission, as Strict and Particular Baptists*, Hadleigh, 1929, reprinted 1945

Philip Reynolds, *These Hundred Years: A Centenary Memento of the Suffolk and Norfolk Association of Strict Baptist Churches*, Ipswich, [1930]

M.S. Ridley (comp.), *'in Memoriam,' containing a Brief Sketch of the Ministerial Life and Labours of the late Rev. Cornelius Elven ... to which is added an Account of the Services held in connection with the Funeral, with the Sermon preached on the following Lord's Day*, 2nd edn, Bury St Edmunds, 1873

Christopher Stell, *An Inventory of Nonconformist Chapels and Meeting-Houses in Eastern England*, Swindon, 2002

Suffolk & Norfolk Association of Strict Baptist Churches, *The Sunday School Branch Silver Jubilee, 1928–1953*, Hadleigh, [1953]

T.C.B. Timmins (ed.), *Suffolk Returns from the Census of Religious Worship of 1851*, Suffolk Record Society 39, Woodbridge, 1997

Norma Virgoe and Tom Williamson (eds), *Religious Dissent in East Anglia: Historical Perspectives*, Norwich, 1993

S.D. Wall et al., *Maidstone Road Baptist Church, Felixstowe, Ter-Jubilee 1808–1958*, n.pl.: n.p., [1958]

S. Wolstenholme, *These Hundred and Fifty Years: A Commemorative Memento of the Suffolk and Norfolk Association of Strict Baptist Churches*, Rowhedge, [1980]

Also issues of the following directories and periodicals:

Circular letters for the Norfolk & Suffolk Association [the 'old association']

Circular letters (later handbooks) for the Suffolk & Norfolk Association [the 'new association']

Baptist Annual Register

Baptist Handbook

Baptist Magazine

Earthen Vessel

Gospel Herald

Gospel Standard

Grace Magazine

Kelly's Directory

Strict Baptist Directory

Suffolk & Norfolk Baptist Home Missionary Union Reports

White's Directory

Websites

'Wangford Village Picture Tour', www.wangford.net/photos/tour-3.php, accessed 29 May 2012

www.britishlistedbuildings.co.uk, accessed 30 May 2012

www.old-maps.co.uk, accessed 4 July 2012 onwards